write
right
right
now

THE BOOK

WALTER M. PERKINS

Published by
Information Plus Professional Services
P.O. Box 1052
Park Forest, IL 60466

Graphic Design by GARGOYLE CREATIVE
Printed in the United States of America

Library of Congress Control Number: 2013938895
ISBN 978-0-615-80750-8

First Edition, 2013

write
right
right
now

THE BOOK

WALTER M. PERKINS

Why Write Right - Right Now - The Book?

I wrote this book to fill two glaring needs in the market place.

First, too many people want to write a book but never do so because they don't know where to begin. Then you have those who write books without seeking advice.

Second, in this still bad economy, thousands have been permanently removed from the traditional job market. Needing to survive economically, the smart ones have started small businesses. But, how do you separate yourself from all others who have done the same thing? How do you position yourself as a **subject-matter expert***?*

Easy, write a book.

Write Right - Right Now - The Book *provides critical information to both of these vast audiences.*

Walter M. Perkins
July 25, 2013

I. ACKNOWLEDGEMENTS

Write Right - Right Now - The Book has been on my mind for a long time. As a professional writer, I buy and read many books and periodicals on the subject of writing. Some of them are mentioned in the **Best Resource Guide**, which can be found in the back of this book.

As a professional, what truly sets you apart from a non-professional is your ongoing desire to get better. This is true no matter what your profession. As noted in **Write Right**, the two best ways to become a better writer are to **read good writing** and **write**.

Despite the many, many books on writing, I wrote this book because numerous people have informed me of their desire to write a book. For various reasons, they want to write a book. However, no one seems to know how to get started.

Write Right is all about getting started and how to proceed, all the way to publication. I am realistic when I say you're not likely to become rich or famous. I am telling the truth when I warn that you'd better like yourself because you're going to spend a lot of time by yourself when writing your book.

Going forward, when people tell me that they want to write a book, I can tell them to go and buy **Write Right**. It will at least get them started and answer a lot of their questions.

I couldn't have done this by myself. I would first like to thank my daughters, **Nia**, the **veterinarian; Patrice,** the **attorney** and **co-editor**; and my wife **Faye,** the **educator**. Each, in her unique way, is responsible and can take credit for the success of this work.

I would also like to thank friends, **Kelly** and, especially **Keith Evans** for helping me lend some authenticity to the chapter dealing with the **IRS; Michelle Thompson**, for serving as co-editor; **Atty. Victor P. Henderson**, for his sterling testimonial; and, I can't forget **graphic designer, Sean Hicks**, for his outstanding design and attention to detail, giving the book the professional look and feel that I was seeking.

Also, thank you to the many people who signed up at writerightthebook.com to receive access to the free writing tips, offered by **Write Right - The Calendar**. Subscribers will continue to receive monthly tips for the rest of the year. My plan is to make the entire calendar available, hopefully as early as **2014**. Also, look for information on **Write Right - The Seminars** and **Write Right - The Workbook**.

Finally, I would like to thank all of the people who indulged me as I repeatedly told them about this great book I was writing.

Here it is.

Walter M. Perkins
April 11, 2013

II. AUTHOR WALTER M. PERKINS

I have been writing for publication for more than 30 years, mostly for national magazines and trade publications. Periodicals include: *"Nation's Business," "Today's Education," "Graduating Engineer," "The Chicago Reporter," "N'DIGO," "The Quill," "The National Black MBA Magazine,"* and many others.

I have also ghost written pieces for the *"Harvard Business Review,"* and *"Vital Speeches of the Day."* In addition, I am the founding editor of *"Operation PUSH Magazine,"* and *"The 100 Magazine,"* formerly the official, national publication of the 100 Black Men of America.

My journalism career includes interviews with Rosa Parks, Walter Cronkite, Smokey Robinson, Professor Harold Cruse, Congressman John Lewis, Quincy Jones, Andrew Brimmer, Linyard Pindling, former prime minister of The Bahamas, and many other influential celebrities and newsmakers.

III. INTRODUCTION

Like most writers, my big dream has been to write a book. I have had many starts and stops along the way. But this time, I have finished.

The two biggest reasons (or excuses) for failing to finish a manuscript are lack of time and focus.

Starting is easy. Finishing is not.

Once you learn the process of writing for magazines, things are easier. You are a proven talent. You know how to meet deadlines. You have contacts in the industry. You know how to research the market. You know how to prepare a query letter, who to send it to, as well as how and when to follow up.

Most importantly, you know, up front, how much you are going to get paid and, usually, the time frame for payment. Hopefully, you have a written contract. You probably don't need an agent at this point.

The problem is that making a living writing for magazines is a long, arduous process.

This is especially true unless you can break into the market that pays the big bucks per article…$1,500 and up. Even then, you must have simultaneous contracts to make a comfortable living. This is especially true if you have shed your 9-5 gig. But, magazine writing is another book.

Even as I write this, I've got at least four unfinished book projects screaming for my attention.

One of the big challenges to finishing and then publishing book manuscripts is the reality of the marketplace. It is very difficult for an unpublished author to write a book, get it published and distributed by a major publisher.

If this happens at all, it is usually with the assistance of an agent.

Typically, successful agents are leery of unpublished authors. If they're going to pitch a product, then they'd rather pitch a known entity. Pitching for a known entity makes it easier to get paid.

A major reason for the recent explosion of **self-publishing** and **smaller publishers** is the difficulty associated with breaking into the mainstream publishing market. Self-publishing and small publishers provide unpublished authors with viable options the first time around. Self-publishing is not the same as vanity publishing. The distinctions between these two forms of pub-lishing will be discussed later in the book.

Often, first-time authors, convinced that the world is waiting for their musings, take the time and expense to pen a manuscript. Much later, they discover that there is no interest or market for what they have written.

This approach to writing a book is called writing on **speculation**, which I do not recommend.

The marketing research effort should precede the writing process when you are preparing to write a book. If the marketing research indicates that there is either no interest in your idea or that the market is saturated with similar books, then you should come up with another idea. Don't waste time researching and writing a book that you cannot sell. More about this later.

Recently, I was blessed with my first contract to write a book.

No, not this one.

What's interesting is that I was able to secure this contract with little effort and no competition from other writers.

I do believe that some things are just meant to happen.

Briefly, the book covers the 50-year history of an organization founded in 1962. What is interesting is that some time ago, while attending the group's 47th convention to begin interviewing some of the founding members, one of the founders decided to interview me.

After thoughtfully considering my credentials, he asked, "Have you ever written a book?" Although it was a fair question, it caught me off guard. I answered truthfully, "No." I then proceeded to interview him and each of the other living founders.

Afterward, I thought about his question. In doing so, I considered why I had never completed what I had started. Without question, each project was important to me when I began. They remain important, even as I write this book.

Why? Read on.

Recently, I attended a small business entrepreneurial institute. The seminar leader began the session by asking who had written a book. Out of about 20 attendees, no one responded. I started to give an explanation of my starts and stops, but decided not to because of time constraints and, probably, interest constraints by the audience.

Toward the end of the two-hour seminar, the presenter challenged the audience to write a book "in the next 90 days."

"If you don't, then you've wasted your time and money," he said.

Not wanting to waste time or money, I embraced the challenge. After perusing my considerable mass of unfinished manuscripts, I decided to write this book. What better project to jump start my book-writing career, than to write a book about how to start, finish, publish and distribute a book?

The 90 days was a benchmark. I actually finished in 89 days. No, really, it took me 89 days to write the first draft, which is the first step in the book-writing process.

That's my story. What's yours?

Author's Note: The author's first book, "Groove Phi Groove, Social Fellowship, Inc. - Black & White Works: The First 50 Years: 1962-2012," was published in 2011. A second edition was published in October 2012, celebrating the organization's 50th anniversary at Morgan State University in Baltimore, site of their founding on October 12, 1962.

An Authoritative Insider's Guide
To Writing For Publication.

I. ACKNOWLEDGEMENTS

II. ABOUT THE AUTHOR

III. INTRODUCTION

IV. TABLE OF CONTENTS

1.
WHY WRITE A BOOK?

*"If there is a book that you want to read
and it hasn't been written yet, then you must write it."*

Toni Morrison - Winner
Nobel Prize in Literature 1993

There are many people who view writing as an exercise that is both mentally and physically painful. That's why so many of us can't write. If this statement is true, then why are so many books being written and published?

In fact, more books are currently being written and published than at any time in history.

In 2010, the latest year available, more than **328,000** titles were published in the United States. This information is according to the **United Nations Educational, Scientific and Cultural Organization (UNESCO),** which monitors the number of books published per year and country as a way to track educational and cultural standards.

Yet, the average person puts writing near the end of the list of things that he or she would like to do. It probably ranks right behind reading; although, I don't have any scientific proof that this statement is true.

What is true is that the acts of reading and writing are inextricably intertwined. Say what? I mean they are irrevocably related. Huh?

Good readers tend to be better writers than non-readers, or those who only read periodically, or when necessary. When you run across a person who writes well, they tend to be voracious readers. What? Okay, they tend to read a lot. They not only read a lot, they enjoy the analytical process associated with reading.

To get back to my original question: **'Why Write a Book?'** People do it for different reasons. Some have specialized information, or a skill that they want to share. Others write for ego purposes. In their minds, even a bad book puts them a step ahead of those who have written no book at all.

If this is your mindset, then stop before you start. Your reason for writing your book is probably the wrong one. And, if your book is poorly written, illogical, grammatically inconsistent, sloppy with the facts, and filled with inaccuracies, and unfulfilled promises, you're probably better off spending your time watching reruns of *"The Lone Ranger,"* or if you really have time on your hands, reading **War and Peace.**

Others write because they think they're smarter than everyone else and, dammit, it's time the world knew it.

Still, others write for publication because of the probably mistaken notion that they are going to become rich and/or famous. Let's face it, if I can get rich, then I don't care if I'm famous or not.

Wrong. This is probably not going to happen; although, it might. The fact is that **90 percent** of the books published are written by **10 percent** of the authors. The other **10 percent** of books published, in any given year, are written by the remaining **90 percent** of authors.

1. Why Write A Book?

Let's be real given the odds of becoming one of the 10 percent who writes 90 percent of books published; which category do you think you will fall into? Yet, still we write.

Let's look at the facts. When you decide to write a book, what can you expect?

For starters, plan to spend a lot of time alone. Picture a person in prison who has been sentenced to three consecutive life terms in solitary confinement. Solitary confinement means you're locked away for as long as 23 hours a day, every day.

The only human contact is the two or, if you're lucky, three times a day that a guard tosses you a bowl of gruel. You shower twice a week, if you're lucky. You get visitors once a month, if you're lucky. And, you're allowed to use the phone once a week, if you're lucky.

Under this set of circumstances, you must get used to hearing the melodic sound of dial tones because nobody on the outside is sitting around waiting to receive your collect calls.

As bleak as this sounds, the multiple lifer probably has a better chance of successfully writing a book than you. This is the case because he has something that you can't seem to find enough of...**time**.

In addition to putting yourself in a voluntary, solitary state for long periods of time, you must eliminate all distractions. As connected as you might be, get unconnected. This means that you must intentionally disconnect all cell phones, beepers, friends, neighbors, bill collectors, and the like.

For long periods of time, you must eliminate all possible **distractions**. If you don't, then they will become the ever-existing excuses for not finishing your book. Even worse, they may become excuses for failing to begin the manuscript for which everyone awaits.

Don't tell anyone you're writing a book. By telling people that you are writing a book, you simply put too much pressure on yourself. Telling acquaintances you are writing a book and either failing to write it or not finishing it within a certain time frame simply gives people too much ammunition for criticism, which you don't need.

Writing a book that never gets finished, let alone published, sets you up as the ultimate non-achiever, even to those who want you to be successful.

As much as it might make you feel good initially; I assure you that it's only temporary. What you do for a living will come up eventually. When it does, your off-the-wall explanation of an unfinished book project will take almost as long as actually writing the book.

Believe me, I know.

I repeat. Keep the fact that you are writing a book a closely held secret, only given out on a **need-to-know** basis.

So, having said all of this, if you're still with me, I still strongly believe that…

The only thing between you and a *New York Times* best Seller is YOU! So…get out of the way and write that BEST SELLER!

Write your book because you have something to say in a unique way.

Write your book because you have knowledge that can help someone, in a meaningful way.

Write your book to entertain. Write your book to teach.

Write your book as a therapeutic exercise that allows you an opportunity to solve a problem or problems that others might also be trying to sort through.

Finally, write your book because it hasn't been written and it's a book that can't be written by anyone but you.

A. Who Should Read This Book?

Anyone who has ever read a book and thought, "I can do better than that," should read this book.

Anyone who wants the immense satisfaction of having written, but not published, or who has almost written a book, should read this book.

Anyone who has specialized knowledge that they've always wanted to share should read this book.

Finally, anyone who loves the written word and has always wanted to write a book, but didn't know how to go about it, should read this book.

B. Why You Should Read This Book:

There is a writer within all of us. That innate skill resides deeper in some of us than others.

Many people who are highly intelligent and possess multiple skill sets, often avoid writing except when they are compelled to do so.

The most important theory behind this book is that most people don't like to write, mostly, because of how they were taught writing when they were in school.

I remember that the conjugating of verbs, diagramming of sentences, rote memorization of grammar rules, and other time-wasting tasks, often left little time for **writing**, which was supposed to be the end result.

I remember, in middle school, being exposed to an English teacher who, in retrospect, probably should have been in therapy. As a matter of course, students were required to keep the front, left leg of their desks balanced on a thumb tack. If the desks slid off the thumb tack, then students were punished.

Imagine trying to learn the basics of English – grammar and sentence structure – while concentrating on balancing the leg of your desk on a thumb tack.

Punishment ranged from major timewasters, like writing lines on the blackboard, to more draconian acts of being closed in an airless closet or forced to stand in a corner wearing a cardboard dunce cap.

Talk about **educational malpractice**.

Students yearned to simply be yelled at for what were usually minor transgressions.

Is it any wonder, given these and similar experiences, that many students would rather experience water boarding, than write? Over time, the writing experience, for many, became synonymous with pain.

The truth is, most people are better writers than they think. They simply have not recovered from the educational mishaps of their youth. Once recovered, they can resume their lives, enjoying their newly found gift of **written literacy**.

Get even...don't curse your former educational tormentors. Learn to write, and then **write and publish your very own book**.

1. Why Write A Book?

2.
HOW DO YOU GET STARTED?

"Like the Devil, the challenge not to write,
will don many different disguises."

Walter M. Perkins - Author
"Write Right - Right Now - The Book"

Getting started. This will be your biggest challenge because there are so many reasons not to get started. Excuses will all strike at the same time, once you decide to write a book.

Face this challenge as soon as it is revealed. It won't be easy. Like the Devil, the challenge not to write, will don many different disguises.

Here are the **Top 5 challenges** you must overcome in order to write your first book.

1. **I DON'T HAVE TIME.** Wrong. You may not have the desire. You may not have the guts. You may not have the stick-toitiveness. Is that a word? It doesn't matter, if you don't have it, then you won't be successful.

If you read the biographies of some of the world's greatest writers, you will find that they found time to write, regardless of their personal circumstances. Some managed to write while laboring under the most challenging circumstances...poverty, imprisonment, and various types of disabilities.

A person who really wants to write will find the time. If you don't believe me, then mentally walk through your typical 24-hour day. Note how much time you waste during that day. Even further, note the various ways that you waste time. Now, add up that time. You will discover that you waste anywhere from an hour to several hours. This is time that you can use to write your book.

For example, the typical adult watches television more than 30 hours a week. Men checked in at just over four and a half hours a day and women watched a little more than five hours daily. These are the numbers, as recently as 2007, according to **Nielsen Media Research**. Cut that time in half. Is that enough time to at least begin your writing project? Sure it is.

Alright, you're hooked on television and you can't see how you're going to survive if you cut your viewing time in half. That's okay. Cut it by a third or quarter. It really doesn't matter how much time you spend writing per day, week, or month.

What is important is that you commit to a regular schedule. Miss a day? Don't worry about it. Just return to your schedule as soon as possible. What's important is the routine.

In many ways, it's just like starting to exercise. Once you work it into your schedule, it's like you've always done it.

Remember, you regularly do the things that are most important to you.

Make writing part of that must-do routine, part of your 24-hour cycle every day.

I single out elimination of television viewing as a major way to free up time, because most of us are victims, one way or another.

Other potential time wasters include:
- Talking on the phone
- Daydreaming
- Shopping when you don't need anything

There are many others that I won't mention. I think you get the idea.

Activities that are an important and necessary part of your daily routine should be continued. For example, don't confuse daydreaming with meditating for spiritual insight and relaxation.

In time, writing will become an enjoyable part of your day. Some even look forward to writing as a form of therapy. And, it's free.

2. **I DON'T KNOW WHAT TO WRITE ABOUT.** Everyone is an expert at something. Figure out your special expertise. Expand your knowledge and start writing.

3. **I HAVE NEVER WRITTEN FOR PUBLICATION.** At one time Stephen King, Richard Wright, James Patterson, Toni Morrison, William Shakespeare, Walter Mosley, Terri McMillan and E. Lynn Harris could all hang their hats on this lame excuse.

How do you like them now?

4. **I HAVE NEVER TAKEN WRITING CLASSES.** Marc McCutcheon wrote a top selling book titled, ***Damn! Why Didn't I Write That?*** He describes how people off the street who had never taken a journalism class, or even gone to college, are making $100,000 or more by turning their ideas into best-selling books.

If they can, you can too.

5. WHO WOULD BE INTERESTED IN WHAT I WRITE? Nobody, if you don't change your attitude. Let's be real. You've got to have a certain level of ego to write a book. If you don't have what it takes, then return this book and get your money back.

I hope you saved your receipt.

WHAT'S NEXT?

I'm assuming you decided to keep the book, if you're reading this far. Now that you've decided to skip the excuses, what should you do next?

Most importantly, develop a table of contents and chapter outline. The table of contents is a simple listing of each chapter and sub-chapter. The chapter outline describes each chapter, giving needed detail. Publishers usually require this as part of your book proposal in order to ensure that you've thoroughly thought about your subject.

1. **DESIGNATE A SPECIFIC TIME AND TIME FRAME TO WRITE EACH DAY.** If you decide to write for 2 hours daily and, after 90 minutes on some occasions, you run out of steam or things to say, don't worry about it. Wrap it up and start fresh the next day. The reality is that you will write more on some days than you will write on other days.

   Don't worry, writing is not a science; it's a process. Once you settle into a schedule, you will find that time spent is increasingly productive. Don't waste time watching the clock.

   When you run out of interesting things to say, call it a day.

2. **FIND A COMFORTABLE PLACE TO WRITE WHERE YOU WON'T BE DISTURBED.** If possible, use this same space everyday. Except for emergencies, make this place off limits to everyone. In the beginning, family members and/or friends will test your seriousness.

   Be firm, this is your time and space. This means no distractions allowed.

3. **GATHER EVERYTHING YOU NEED.** Before you settle into your writing space, make sure you have what you need to be productive. That means everything. I'm talking about flash drives, paper, snacks, water, juice, whatever you need.

   The worse use of your time is to spend it jumping up and down, roaming back and forth, looking for things you could and should have gathered, before you sat down to write.

   While you are an adult and can make your own decisions, **I do not recommend that you drink alcohol, or ingest any other substances, hallucinogens, or the like at this time.**

   I would suggest that you want to be entirely lucid at this time. Your mind should be focused, disciplined, and sober.

4. **DON'T TRY TO DO TOO MUCH IN ONE SITTING.** This will only frustrate you. Once you settle into a routine, time passes quickly. Sit down at the start of the month. Divide each week and every day into weeks and days that are based on what you want to get done.

   This way, if you fall short on a particular day or days, then it is easy to catch up because you know where you started and you know where you want to be by the end of the month.

5. **BE YOUR OWN WORST CRITIC.** You will become a better writer faster if you set high standards. Be sure you are satisfied with what you produce before showing it to anyone.

Don't get mad and go running and screaming from your house, if your family and friends don't love your writing, as much as you do. Remember, this is where you live, and you eventually have to return.

Now, you're good to go. I've at least got you off the ledge, where most new writers lurk. You're now sitting with your flash drive, water, and fruit, staring hard at a blank computer screen.

You're all pumped up and ready to go. You feel good. You've decided to write that *New York Times* **Best Seller.** This is your first time around the track.

"I didn't know it was going to be this easy," you say to yourself.

Hah, think again.

Now it's time to face a new challenge.

2. How Do You Get Started?

3.
DOES IT MATTER IF YOU'VE NEVER WRITTEN FOR PUBLICATION?

*"Writing well for publication demands first,
that you pick a subject that excites you and will attract others."*

Judith Appelbaum - Author
"How To Get Happily Published"

No. It does not matter that you have never written for publication.

Publication experience does not matter as much as proper preparation.

Most beginning writers have no idea what they are doing. The only thing certain is their desire to write. They may want to write a magazine article. They may want to write a book. They may even want to write their names in wet concrete and watch it dry.

For just a moment, let's consider the fact that I can't swim. It's not that I never had a desire to swim. It's just that I never learned the right way. Therefore, I can assure you that if you ever read or hear about me washing up on the shore of a deep body of water, it won't be because I jumped into the water.

People spend their time doing what's important to them. Swimming, as important of a life skill as it is, never made it to the top of my priority list.

Most people feel the same about writing. As important of a life skill as it is, it usually does not make the **Top 10** list of must-do things. The fact that you are making your way through this book means that you are not one of these people.

Getting back to my original question: Does it matter if you've never written for publication?

It is important to note that just like there was a pre-sex period in everyone's life, pre- as in before; there was a pre-publication period in every writer's life. This is the case for every published writer, no matter how famous or accomplished.

Every writer went through a period, sometimes extended period, of pre-publication.

At the point when aspiring writers decide the published word is their calling, they begin learning more about what they are about to get into. This means learning the craft and business of writing. For, unless you are writing for yourself, the reading public be damned, writing is indeed a business.

If you come up with a good idea that you are able to weave into a professional manuscript, then publishers give nary a thought whether you have previously published.

A published author has one important advantage over a new author. This advantage is name recognition. And, if their book or books are successful, they have another advantage over new authors; specifically, they have money in the bank and, maybe, a contract and advance to write another book.

If their efforts result in best seller success, they most likely will receive an advance plus a long-term contract to write more books.

3. Does It Matter If You've Never Written For Publication?

But, it all begins with a good idea that evolves into a well written, published and marketed publication. Perhaps I should say marketed and published because **the marketing strategy** should begin at about the same time the idea is developed.

A well-written and published book without a well-developed marketing plan is a waste of time, unless you are just writing for yourself, friends, and family.

If you think people are going to buy your book just because you wrote it, think again. Even name authors need a good marketing and distribution plan.

Yale Law Professor Stephen Carter knows what I am talking about. No stranger to the good life, Carter has carved out an enviable literary reputation by writing about the sometimes devious hi-jinks of New England's African American upper crust, of which he has intimate, first-hand knowledge.

The author of numerous non-fiction books, the best selling, *The Emperor of Ocean Park,* was his first try at fiction.

A book that wasn't so much read as experienced, *Ocean Park* was a runaway best seller, probably making it unnecessary for the esteemed law professor to ever again have to smack a nodding law student upside the head in order to gain the student's attention in the middle of one of his lectures.

Key to the book's success was a well-executed marketing plan by publisher **Vintage Books (a subdivision of Random House)**, This plan resulted in *Ocean Park* earning *New York Times* Best Seller status and multiple printings.

USA Today's Deirdre Donahue wrote, *"I haven't inhaled a novel so rich, rewarding, and compelling since Tom Wolfe's "A Man in Fall,"... The mystery aspects had me reading the book at stop signs while driving."*

I agree that *Ocean Park* was a thoroughly engrossing, intelligent and entertaining read. So much so that I would have bought his next book even if it had been written in Chinese, a language I can neither read, speak, nor write. And, so I did, to my profound disappointment…

It's not that **New England White** was a bad book. It's just that **Ocean Park** was so good that it was difficult to top. That's where I feel Carter made his mistake. He probably felt that he had to top his first effort. He should not have felt that way. A good second novel would have satisfied all, but the most critical of his fans.

Even so, the Boston Globe called his second book, *"the eagerly awaited, electrifying new novel from the author of **The Emperor of Ocean Park,** a rip-roaring entertainment."*

My point here is that Carter, previously untested as a fiction writer, shot to the top of the heap with his first novel. Along the way, he inspired favorable comparisons to Theodore Dreiser, Tom Wolfe, and others.

He was successful because he had a good idea. He wrote about a subject, the black, upper-middle and upper class, that he knew about so well. It is also a subject that has not been explored nearly as much as the so-called black, lower or underclass (under what?), but, you get what I mean.

If Carter can do it, then so can you. Just prepare yourself as the professor did. Success as a law professor didn't automatically mean that he would be successful as a first time fiction writer. **Excellent writing, plot, character development**, combined with a **well-executed marketing plan**, helped ensure his success.

Also, successfully publishing several non-fiction books did not automatically translate into the type of best seller success he experienced with his first novel.

So, no, you don't need publishing experience to publish successfully. **You need**:

- **A good idea**
- **A table of contents**
- **Descriptive chapter outlines**
- **Developed writing skills**
- **An understanding and execution of marketing**
- **Knowledge of your audience(s)**
- **Knowledge of your competition**

4.
WHAT DO YOU WANT TO WRITE ABOUT?

"Writing comes more easily if you have something to say."

Sholem Asch - Author

Let's do a quick review of all the books that have ever been written. To my knowledge, the only one published without a stated subject was, *The Nothing Book.*

Recalling from what sometimes is a dim memory *The Nothing Book* was a bound book of blank pages designed to be filled in by you, the unwitting dupe who bought the book.

The people who put this together followed all but one of the rules listed in Chapter 3, **developed writing skills**.

The Nothing Book was a **good idea**. The perpetrators **understood both marketing** and **their audiences**. They also knew all they needed to know about their **competition**. There was none.

A Good Idea

If you are going to write and publish a book, then you must begin with a good idea. It doesn't have to necessarily be an original idea, just a good idea. It could be an old idea with a different twist. You discover and write about a new use for an old product, for example.

How do you come up with a good idea? Easy, they are everywhere. First, take a personal inventory.

- **What are you good at?**
- **What do you like to do...hobbies, specialized interests?**
- **What professional skills have you developed?**
- **What kinds of advice do you give to others?**
- **What do others think you are good at doing?**
- **What can't you do that you would like to do?**
- **What don't you know that you would like to know?**

While it's much easier to write about something you know about, it's a greater challenge to choose a subject you don't know much about; experience it and learn more about it.

Writers and even would-be writers are curious about everything. They want to know how things work and why. They don't take anyone's word for anything. Some would call them the ultimate cynics.

As I write this on **Friday, June 26, 2009**, the whole world is mourning the untimely death of **Michael Jackson**. Michael, the musical icon and global humanitarian that he was, has, upon his passing, united much of the world in collective, reflective grief.

His celebrity and, ultimately, his immense legacy are touching people across geographic, ethnic, religious, gender, generational, and economic boundaries.

On yesterday, Thursday, June 25, 2009, I watched a television interview with Rudy Clay, mayor of Gary, Indiana, hometown of Michael and the rest of the Jacksons. The interview was about Michael Jackson.

Much later, during the same newscast, it was reported that the body of what was believed to be the remains of Jada Justice, a two-year-old youngster of Hispanic and African American origin who had been missing for two weeks, had been found.

Jada was also from Gary, Indiana.

However, the mayor of Gary was not asked about Jada Justice.

While the whole world is preoccupied with the passing of Michael Jackson, only a few of those people have ever heard of Jada Justice.

My point here is while thousands of writers will be pursuing Michael Jackson stories, who will write about Jada Justice?

While she was not an internationally known celebrity, she had a story to tell as well.

If you are going to become a successful, published writer, then you must be able to discern the human interest stories that lurk behind people like Jada Justice.

- **Who was she...likes, dislikes, special talents?**
- **What happened to her and why?**
- **Who is responsible and why?**
- **How can such tragedies be prevented?**
- **Why are such tragedies increasing?**

Undoubtedly, someone, perhaps multiple people, will be caught, charged and tried in this heinous case. This will produce additional story lines for the industrious writer.

Author's Note: In August 2010 "A Hobart, Ind., woman was convicted of murder in the beating death of her two-year old cousin." That cousin was Jada Justice.

Source: Post-Tribune and Sun-Times Media Wire

This is just one example of how a good idea can be developed from current events. It doesn't have to be a tragedy. It can be a good news story like the following:

Several years ago, someone told me an interesting story that turned out to be true. There was a family of three or four daughters being raised by a single mother on Chicago's South Side.

Unfortunately, as is the case too often, it doesn't really matter what happened to the father. Or, there might have been more than one father. Truth be told, African American males have been so trivialized and marginalized in this society that the plight of the male or males in this particular story is unfortunately not important.

Anyway, as fate would have it, the hardworking mother dies.

Rather than notify the various social service agencies assigned to the family, the oldest daughter stepped in and began raising her younger sisters.

Meanwhile, she graduates from college, later gaining acceptance to a prestigious Midwestern medical school.

All the while, she continues raising and attending to the needs of her siblings.

As the tale winds down, the young lady graduates from medical school with her young family intact. She is now reportedly a licensed medical doctor.

This is a story screaming for a skilled writer, published or not. The human interest elements are numerous and obvious.

- **Why did she do what she did?**
- **How was she able to pull it off?**

- Was she assisted in any way by sympathetic social workers?
- Did she ever confide in anyone?
- Did she have any close calls?
- How did the sisters turn out?
- Would she do it again?
- If so, what would she do differently?

These are just a couple of off-the-top examples that demonstrate the ease with coming up with doable and marketable ideas for your book.

Caution.

If you have a lazy mind fueled by a lackluster imagination that sees the world in black and white, instead of technicolor, then you might want to find a historic building being restored to its original splendor and apply for a job as an elevator operator.

Good Ideas: How Are They Developed?

By now, you should begin to see an image developing of a **successful writer**. In fact, that writer should look something like you. Let's check and be sure.

The **successful writer** is:

- Curious
- Observant
- Creative
- Imaginative
- A reader
- A listener
- A researcher
- A traveler
- Open-minded
- Morally & ethically centered
- Knowledgeable about the law
- Not afraid to be wrong

Above all, the **successful writer** is a **thinker**, willing to turn ideas inside out in order to reach conclusions that are not necessarily shared by the rank-and-file.

I once got into a serious argument with someone when I challenged his belief that the main purpose of a college education is to graduate and get a good job. If you do a poll, you will no doubt discover that this person's opinion prevails among most college graduates.

However, I incurred this person's wrath by suggesting that the main purpose of a college education should be to enhance a person's ability to think, solve problems, and stake out consistently moral and ethically defensible positions.

Despite the fact that a college degree will no doubt help you make more money over a lifetime of toiling on someone else's behalf, it is my belief that economics is not the main purpose.

Whether a college grad or not (consider that some of the most celebrated writers are not) to be successful at this game, you must be willing to think, no matter how painful it might be.

Remember, once you begin the process, the easy or first answer, approach or solution is not always the best. Once you have trained yourself to think, you will discover that often answers to complex problems just pop into your head.

This is the case because your subconscious is awake. It is working to help you reach a reasonable solution, even as you sleep.

That's how powerful your mind is. Just allow it to work for you!

More About Idea Development

Ideas that can later be developed into published articles and/or books, often come from everyday circumstances.

For example, what is more routine than visiting a fast food restaurant and eating items that exceed the minimum daily recommendations for salt, sugar, cholesterol and fat?

When this type of food is consumed on a regular basis, it can contribute to a person suffering a stroke, having a heart attack, developing diabetes, or even dying prematurely.

Despite my deep desire to name names, no names shall be mentioned. **You will find out why when you get to the chapter on legal issues.**

One bright Saturday morning, I found myself standing in line at one of these establishments.

Why? Because it's fast, convenient and cheap. And, if you must know, I didn't have much time, money or gas. That's why I was there.

Okay?

Once seated, I happened to notice a young family. We'll call them the **Overweights**. As we often find in the 21st century, what we call a family often consists of a mother and an undetermined number of children; in this case, there were three children.

Mrs. or Ms. Overweight was, of course, overweight, as were her two daughters, both apparently teenagers. The youngest, a male, appeared to be 4-6 years old, his young pores not yet afflicted with excess fat and grease.

But, not to worry. In between fast and furious bites of her food, Overweight was force feeding French fries to her young son. Alternately, the mother and two teenagers were giving the boy bites from their sandwiches.

I glanced at my watch. It had just struck 11, a.m. that is.

My ever-fertile writer's mind fast-forwarded a few years to when this young man, now in his early teens, will be burdened with his own supply of fat and grease. I then imagined him a few years later, repeating these acts of **parental malpractice** on his own children.

That's it. While I could do nothing to rescue this young lad from the gastronomic excesses of his mother and sisters, I could, perhaps, bring attention to this growing problem by writing about it within the broader subject of **parental malpractice**.

Where would I start? Is this a new concept? What is the definition of **parental malpractice?** Or, if it is something new, how will I define it? While we can agree that there are acts commonly classified as **parental abuse and neglect**, is gastronomical excess in this category?

Not feeding a child over a period of time, would be considered neglect and, later, abuse, if it continued.

However, is overfeeding a child with food that is not good for them -insofar as it lacks nutrition and damages their future development- parental abuse and/or neglect? Or, is this, and other acts that are indirectly harmful to children, something new...something we can place under the broad title of **parental malpractice?**

Now that my **inquiring mind** has given me this great idea; it's research time to see if it has merit. **I now want to know:**

1. **Is there a recognized concept of parental malpractice?**
2. **Are there any known experts?**
3. **If so, has it been treated as a legal, moral, or ethical concept?**
4. **Is it a concept recognized in the United States, elsewhere?**
5. **Is it a criminal, civil, or administrative concept?**
6. **If criminal, is it typically a felony or misdemeanor?**
7. **What states have taken the lead in developing this as a legal concept?**
8. **What are the penalties, if found guilty of parental malpractice?**

I could ask more questions, but you get the idea. I have taken an everyday occurrence and developed it into a possible story concept, something which could first be developed as an article, and, later, expanded into a book. How about a 50-state reference guide, citing laws and resources in each state?

By the way, **don't steal my idea** because I just might write about this subject. Just kidding, you can steal it since **ideas can't be copyrighted**. But more about that in the legal section. If you write about **parental malpractice**, at least give my book source credit.

Thanks.

See how easy that was?

Not convinced? Let's try another idea.

Every June 19th several states celebrate a day called **Juneteenth**, also known as **"African American Emancipation Day,"** the oldest known celebration of slavery's end.

The **Emancipation Proclamation**, freeing the slaves, was signed into law by President Abraham Lincoln on January 1, 1863. However, it wasn't until June 19, 1865 that General Gordon Granger finally made it to Galveston, Texas with the news that the former slaves were free, and had been for about two and a half years!

This was also apparently the first time that blacks in Galveston knew that General Robert E. Lee had surrendered in April of 1865, ending the Civil War. There have been several explanations for why this happened, all interesting research and writing subjects.

Imagine, you are a former slave on a Texas plantation, who discovers two and a half years after the fact that:

You should have been granted your freedom and weren't because no one bothered to tell you that you were free. Imagine the first conversation you might have had with your now, former slave owner.

What kinds of legal claims might you have against the former master and his estate? Might this be a good time and place to make a compelling argument for **reparations?**

Other things that might spur idea development include:

- **Predictions**
- **Trends**
- **Surveys**
- **Polls**
- **Economic indicators**
- **Current events**

There are many others that will come to mind once you embrace the thinking process. Keep in mind that **travel** is one of the best idea generators. Why? You are exposed to new places, people, food, culture, and artifacts indigenous to your place of travel.

On my first trip to Africa, specifically South Africa, I was amazed that, despite the widespread poverty encountered in many places, we never saw anyone begging.

Coming from a place like Chicago where it is common to see people begging, some of whom are better dressed than I am; I was simply astounded.

As you can see, ideas are everywhere. Just pay attention. Discovering and developing ideas are easy once you focus.

4. What Do You Want To Write About?

5.

WHO WILL BUY YOUR BOOK?

I will buy your book. No kidding; I will be your first customer if at least two conditions are met:

- **Your book is about something in which I am interested.**
- **I know that your book exists.**

It would help if it is well written as well as grammatically and stylistically consistent. It also helps if it is interesting to read, authoritative, and speaks to my needs as a reader, with timely presented information. If it's professionally designed, then I am pleased.

If your book answers more questions than it raises, or, at least, answers the questions that it raises, then I'll buy an extra copy and give it to a friend. If it contains a helpful resource directory, I'll recommend it to professional colleagues who are interested in the subject.

If your book contains all of these elements and you attend to the essentials of marketing, you've probably got a winner.

But, even if you fail to include all of these elements, showing evidence that you are a good writer, not necessarily a great writer, but a good writer…you must ensure that:

- **Your book is about something in which I am interested.**
- **I know that your book exists.**

I know several writers who have taken valuable time, energy and resources to write and publish a book. It is only then that they discover that there is no interest in what they have written, as it is written.

This means that they have failed to properly research their book idea. Reasons for the lack of interest could be many.

- **Information on the subject could be so available that a book is unnecessary.**
- **Similar books might already saturate the market.**
- **Low sales of previous books on the subject, might indicate a lack of interest.**
- **Those who might have interest in your book do not know it exists.**

There might be many other reasons why the book-buying public has ignored your book.

Now, for the sake of me finishing this chapter in a timely manner, let's assume that demonstrated interest in your work has resulted in sporadic sales, enough for you to at least break even on time, resources, and ego.

This means you have done some of the necessary tasks to find a pool of people interested in spending a few bucks on your hard work.

But, beware. It could also mean that you have exhausted and, probably, exasperated, your already small group of family and friends. Now, while you have the satisfaction of seeing your freshly published book sitting proudly unmolested on various bookshelves, you have probably failed to:

Let the pool of those who might really be interested know that your book exists.

That's why I emphasized earlier the importance of developing a marketing plan at about the same time the book idea pops into your head.

Finding Your Audiences

Ideally, you should be able to pinpoint your audience(s) at the same time you decide that your destiny is to write a book. As I suggested earlier, unless you are writing for yourself to satisfy some unsatisfied or undefined psychological need...translated ego, by now you should have given serious thought to whom the subject matter of your book is directed.

Once the mental process begins, it doesn't have to be painful. You will realize that if your book is worth the time, it will probably appeal to multiple audiences.

It's up to you to find out who and where they are.

Let's start with this book, the one you have in your hand. Who is this book intended to reach?

Obviously, this book was intended for you, since you have thrown down a few bucks for the privilege of reading its contents. Or, someone you know thought you might be interested because of what they know, or what they think they know, about you and your interests.

Right now, next to my family and a few friends, you are the most important person in my universe. You're reading my book.

That means that I did something to identify your interests in the subject matter. Then I did something else to actually bring my book to your attention.

How did I bring you to my book? Well, once I determined that, despite all of the books in print discussing the publication process and how to write a book, this publication was still necessary, I searched out my:

Primary Audience(s)

Primary audience(s) are the people whom I felt could most directly benefit from and who would be most likely to act on the advice given in this book.

They include:

- **People who have dreamed about writing a book, but thought it was either too hard or too much trouble**
- **People who began, but didn't finish, a manuscript because it wasn't high on their priority list of things to do**
- **People who had a good idea, talked it to death, before losing interest and coming up with another good idea, which they also talked to death**
- **People who had good intentions, but had no idea about how to go about the process**
- **People who have expert knowledge and skill about a particular subject, or several subjects, but a psychological fear of the writing process**

All of the above and then some.

Secondary Audience(s)

- Secondary audience(s) are the people, possibly you, who may benefit from this book.

All you need to do is properly prepare yourself.

You've already begun by buying and reading this book.

You will learn how to find and market to your audiences, by following the tips in the **section discussing marketing and distribution.**

6.

WHO IS YOUR COMPETITION?

"Ordinary people can write extraordinary books."

Marc McCutcheon - Author
"Damn! Why Didn't I Write That?"

In the beginning, your main competition is likely to be you. Once you erase all of the barriers to your success, your main competition is likely to be:

- **Similar books promising to treat similar subject matter in a unique way, but failing to deliver**
- **Similar books promising to treat similar subject matter in a unique way that do deliver**
- **Established authors who are demonstrated experts in some subjects, but, not all, and who try to market themselves beyond their expertise**
- **The author who is a marketing expert, but not much else**

The best advice, I can give, is to be aware of your competition, and their differences and similarities to your book.

If a renowned expert on a subject writes something that is the exact opposite of your advice on the same subject, then just be sure that you know what you are talking about.

The worst blow to your professional reputation is to be blindsided or discredited by a known expert.

Many subjects and issues allow for differences of opinion or allow for reasonable people to come to different conclusions, sometimes using the same data.

However, even if you acknowledge that what you are offering is simply your professional opinion, then beware. This is especially true if **your professional opinion** weighs too heavily against what is commonly accepted as fact or truth about a particular subject.

At the very least, **always try to come close to being on the same side as common sense.**

If you have staked out a professional niche as being **"controversial,"** one willing to challenge knowledge commonly accepted as factual…Beware, in your landmark **geographic** and **scientific** tome, of taking the long discredited position that **"the world is flat."**

If you develop a reputation for staking out such outlandish and discredited positions, then your literary oar will be quelled as surely as if you were trying to row your boat in a cement pond.

Being known as controversial is one thing. Being known as an idiot is quite another. If the latter is indeed the case, then it's better to keep it to yourself. Don't write a book, letting everyone know what, up to now, has been a closely held secret, known only to family and close friends.

6. Who Is Your Competition?

7.
WHAT DO YOU NEED TO KNOW ABOUT THE WRITING PROCESS?

"I'm not a very good writer, but I'm an excellent rewriter."

James Michener - Author
"South Pacific"

As a writer, you want to do more than just make it look and sound good. As a writer, you want to write with unambiguous substance.

Make it **understandable**. Make it **meaningful**. Make it **memorable**.

This book is not intended to be a primer on writing. If you are interested in writing and publishing professionally, then certain things are assumed.

Assumptions include that you know the **basics** of:

- **Grammar**
- **Sentence structure**

- **Paragraph structure**
- **Spelling**

Even if the above are not among your skill sets, the good thing about the writing process is that it doesn't matter...**at least not in the beginning.**

When you begin this process, the only thing that matters is that the meanderings you call writing make sense to you. If they don't, you've got a problem.

If your writing does not make sense to you, then you might want to rethink your interest in writing a book. It may not be worth your time, effort, or resources, if you don't have a basic understanding of how the English language is structured to facilitate effective communication.

But, if you're like most of the rest of us who have neither the time nor interest in memorizing a bunch of rules, then keep reading.

The goal here is to remove all blocks–be they real or imagined– to writing. Some of the greatest barriers to writing are fears associated with making typos, spelling mistakes, as well as sentence and paragraph structure.

The dirty little secret of writing is that the first few drafts don't matter. That's why you don't show them to anyone, unless you are a masochist dying to get your feelings hurt.

The good news is that your first few drafts will be read by no one but you, unless you make the mistake of sharing. At this point, you can free yourself of all worry about grammar and all of its related demons. Those demons are of absolutely no importance at this point. With that said, later, grammar becomes very important to the success of your project.

That's why style references and grammar guides are valuable tools for a writer. Trust me, there is a reference or guide for every conceivable grammatical or structural problem. You can study them privately, wherever you write.

7. What Do You Need To Know About The Writing Process?

Successful writers will tell you that what improves their work is constant rewriting and editing.

Only uninformed novices think they can dash off a quick, unedited draft and be finished. It's simply not the way things are done.

If your current writing skills are at least everyday average, there are two ways that you can immediately improve.

- **Read good writing**
- **Write!**

Reading Good Writing

I was fortunate to grow up in a household that had a profound respect for the written word. When books are constant companions, they are less intimidating. I was surrounded by, *The World Book Encyclopedia, Great Books of the Western World,* as well as works by Shakespeare and other classical writers.

I also read Richard Wright, Claude McKay, Zora Neale Hurston, Alexandre Dumas, Chester Himes, Gwendolyn Brooks, Claude Brown, and others.

My constant reading and quest for knowledge, which continues, evolved into an interest in and talent for writing, and later writing for publication.

Along the way, I developed a curiosity as to how and why things work. I became interested in trends and the predictions of futurists, like Alvin Toffler. He has an uncanny knack of accurately telling us what is going to happen 10 years and beyond. Then he writes a book about his predictions.

Toffler is the acclaimed advisor to presidents and other world leaders, and the author of *Future Shock, The Third Wave,* and *Power Shift.* He is a must read for any aspiring writer who wants to have a better understanding of the world in which we live, and credible insight into what's in store.

Reading and writing cannot be separated. One begets the other.

Write!

Once I began writing regularly, I discovered that the more I wrote, the better I became. It's the same as developing any other skill. You must do it to master it, or at least to get better.

Ask world class athletes how they became world class and they will tell you, **"practice."** Ask successful writers how they became successful and they will tell you the same thing.

The simple art of letter writing by hand is practically a forgotten art form. Both technology and personal laziness are to blame.

Simple examination of a well written letter reveals that it is an art form. Grammatically correct, structurally perfect, error free… And, all without spell check, which is one of the greatest inhibitors to literacy since the digital watch.

Try reviving the art by personally sitting down and writing a letter to someone. Do it on a regular basis and see how your writing improves.

Why?

Because, no one wants to come across as illiterate to someone whom they care about. And, you would only take the time to write a letter to someone whose opinion you truly hold in high regard.

Try it, it works.

Now, even after you have taken this advice, you may still need a little help.

Don't let rules get in the way of getting started.

Important Style Tips:

1. When making the first reference to a person, include the full name, plus professional title, when relevant.

2. Never recognize degrees or titles that haven't been earned. Honorary degrees should be explained.

3. When in doubt about proper spelling, look it up.

4. Never guess about the spelling of someone's name.

5. When in doubt about proper word usage, look it up.

6. Substitute small words for large words wherever possible. Example, small not diminutive.

7. Write as concisely as possible. Or, better still, write concisely.

8. Check facts to ensure accuracy, even if you have to check multiple sources.

9. Before letting anyone review your work, check everything for accuracy.

10. Clarity, accuracy and credibility are critical to good writing.

Remember, when writing about a person, place, or event, you should rank order the who, what, when, where, why and how. The significance of the action should be clear to the reader.

All The Grammar You'll Ever Need...And Then Some

When I first thought about writing this book, I vowed to make it easy to navigate. That is, I didn't want to bog it down with a lot of rules of the road, so to speak.

Before you sit down to write, check the **Best Resource Guide** in the appendix of this book for a highly recommended grammar book. Keep it handy so you can check it when absolutely necessary.

Do not, and I repeat, do not allow the grammar guide to be a road block as you develop your manuscript.

Finally, **treat your written words as money.** Use them properly, profitably, and don't waste them.

7. What Do You Need To Know About The Writing Process?

8.
HOW & WHERE DO YOU GET INFORMATION?

"A reporter (writer) can confirm otherwise hidden, complex business and government transactions by researching public records."

William Gaines
Two-time Pulitzer Prize winner for Investigative Reporting

You're in luck. No matter your subject, there's information everywhere. Not long ago you had to actually leave your house, office, or wherever you were crafting your masterpiece, to get information. Back then, the library was an obvious first destination.

Today, assuming you have access to a computer, you need go no further. Even so, I still visit my local library when:

- **I need a quiet place to read and study.**
- **I need to copy material from reference sources that are not convenient to access on the Internet.**
- **I need to make multiple copies of other research material.**

In addition, depending on your subject, the library will have **special** collections, only available at that one site. **University**

libraries are especially helpful.

Influential and famous people often donate their papers to universities, libraries, and museums.

Starting Your Research

Remember, before you actually sit down to write, create an outline. This is especially important if you are writing a book. This is important for a couple of reasons.

1. It helps you focus and think through what you want to write about.
2. A well-conceived outline helps you determine where to find relevant information.

You can locate good information no matter how obscure the subject. It is up to you to judge the credibility of what you find.

For example, at first glance, beware of much of what you find on the Internet. Make sure it is from a credible source. Unfortunately, because of fraud on the World Wide Web, you're not always sure if you have accessed the official site of a person or organization.

If in doubt, it's probably worth the price of a phone call to be absolutely sure.

Nothing harms your credibility as a writer as badly as **wrong information.** It is especially unacceptable since you have ample time to check your sources, Internet and otherwise.

In addition to the popular media, radio, television, magazines, newspapers, and the Internet; the following is a partial list of easily accessible sources:

1. **Government Agencies** - From the federal government, right down to the smallest municipality...a huge amount of free information is available from the federal government's

various agencies in particular. *"Information U.S.A.,"* compiled by well-known author/researcher **Matthew Lesko**, lists everything you need to know about U.S. government resources. Originally published in 1986, it remains a reference worth knowing about, if you can find it. Original **ISBN reference number was 0140467459. Google Matthew Lesko** for information on this and similar publications.

2. **Libraries** - Be aware that there are specialty libraries covering every conceivable subject. They are also often recipients of specialized collections. Go to **Yahoo** and key in **Special Library Collections** for a comprehensive list and links to every library subject category.

3. **Local Chambers of Commerce** - Excellent sources for business information. They also produce business-related publications, and host information seminars that feature business leaders, speaking on various topics.

4. **Local Historical Societies** - They hold important information about their subject areas. These organizations also produce historical publications, newsletters and other informational material. These institutions also often host speakers discussing historical topics.

5. **Museums** - These institutions often contain information and artifacts, not found elsewhere, from the general to the very specific.

6. **Professional Associations** - There is a professional organization for every profession. Because they are mostly advocates for the professions and trades they represent, these groups usually provide a wide range of either free or very low-cost information.

   Many of the largest and most influential professional associations are found in Washington D.C. and Chicago. For example, **The American Bar Association; American Medical Association; American Library Association; and American**

Dental Association are all located in Chicago. The *Encyclopedia of Associations,* available at all major libraries, lists contact information for all major professional associations.

7. **University Libraries** - Repositories of vast amounts of research, regardless of your topic. Many also have special collections, depending on their academic focus and/or specialties.

Beware, many school-based libraries require you to be a graduate or current student, or have some other identifiable, certifiable connection to the institution. The resourceful writer should have no problem gaining access.

Be aware, that in addition to holding special collections and donations, many organizations, especially not-for-profits, use university libraries to professionally organize and archive their public papers and photographs.

A Note About Presidential Libraries - Official & Unofficial - www.archives.gov

There are 13 official Presidential Libraries located across the country. These collections receive their "official" designation, if, and only if, they are operated by the **National Archives and Records Administration.** Those libraries are the following:

1. **George Bush**
2. **George W. Bush**
3. **Jimmy Carter**
4. **William J. Clinton**
5. **Dwight D. Eisenhower**
6. **Gerald R. Ford**
7. **Herbert Hoover**
8. **Lyndon Baines Johnson**
9. **John F. Kennedy**
10. **Richard M. Nixon**
11. **Ronald Reagan**
12. **Franklin D. Roosevelt**
13. **Harry S. Truman**

8. How & Where Do You Get Information?

The following presidents have libraries owned by states, private foundations, or historical societies. They include:

1. **Calvin Coolidge**
2. **Rutherford B. Hayes**
3. **William McKinley**
4. **Abraham Lincoln**
5. **Woodrow Wilson**

To access Calvin Coolidge's library for example, **Google Calvin Coolidge Presidential Library.** Each of the "unofficial" collections can be accessed similarly.

These sources will at least get you started. Once you begin, you will discover leads that will point you in the direction of other useful information.

9.
WHAT OTHER INFORMATION SOURCES WILL YOU USE?

"Researching a topic involves a lot more than scooping up facts and figures off the Internet - Although Internet research can be a good starting point."

Fred White - Author
"the daily writer"

No matter the subject of your writing, much of your information will come from the following sources.

 ## A. The Interview as a Source

The interview, whether in person, by telephone, via e-mail or otherwise, is one of the most valuable information sources at your disposal.

There is always the possibility that an **interviewee** will not tell the truth, depending on the type of information you are seeking; or, he may only tell you part of the truth.

That's okay.

Often there are other people or sources who can prove, disprove, and/or give additional information, leading you closer to what you are seeking.

Undoubtedly, there are also **documents** either readily available, or available via research, the Internet, the **Freedom of Information Act (FOIA)**, and other sources to be discussed.

Even in the case of a **dying declaration**, where a person comes clean as his last earthly act, there is often supporting documentation, to either prove or disprove what the person said.

 # B. Other Sources of Information

Various types of documents, including: public and private records, court transcripts, legislative hearings, books, and the like, are also important.

You may quote at will from documents like the **U.S. Constitution**; but, understand that it is subject to many different interpretations.

Therefore, if you are quoting the Constitution in support of something you are writing, then you may need to include the opinions and interpretations of recognized experts on the particular section about which you are writing.

Even if **you, the writer**, are a **recognized expert on the subject,** you add to your credibility by including the opinions of other recognized experts, even if they disagree with your position.

Other Credible Information Sources
- **Surveys**
- **Polls**
- **Criminal & civil trial records**
- **Bankruptcy records**
- **Divorce actions**
- **Government bids & contracts**
- **Government grant & loan information**
- **Declassified information**

Also:

Records of **real estate transactions including:**
- **Mortgages**
- **Liens**
- **Foreclosures**
- **Deed in lieu of foreclosure**

And:

IRS Form 990

This is a public document revealing how **not-for-profit organizations** are spending their money. It also helps you determine whether they are adhering, to the rules governing their not-for-profit status.

Churches must also file this document.

In addition, depending on what you are writing about, much public information is available from:
- **Better Business Bureaus**
- **State, county & local governments**
- **Congressional offices**
- **Public interest organizations**
- **Business & professional associations**
- **Professional licensing agencies**
- **Medicare & Medicaid medical financial reports**
- **Building inspection reports**
- **Public facility records**
- **School records**
- **Other government agencies**

On a more personal level, don't overlook:
- **Letters**
- **Journals**
- **Diaries**
- **Memoirs by current & former government officials, and other public figures**
- **Informal notes**

Compilation of a complete list, covering each and every information interest, is an impossible and unnecessary task. These sources are more than enough to get you going, no matter your information interest.

You will find that once you open one information door, others will reveal themselves, eager to share what's inside.

C. Freedom of Information Act (FOIA)

For a wide range of available sources, Google Freedom of Information Act.

Consider FOIA a research tool of last resort because it can be time-consuming and costly. Generally, the FOIA requires all federal agencies to disclose agency records when requested in writing, by any person.

FOIA does not cover Congress or the federal judiciary. Each state has enacted its own public information law and should be consulted individually.

Major difficulties in actually getting information under the FOIA are the **nine exemptions** and **three exclusions**. For example, any records related to personnel issues are routinely exempted under FOIA and state statutes.

D. Still More Information Sources

Government Accounting Office (GAO) - www.gao.gov

The "Congressional Watchdog" investigates and keeps track of how the federal government spends taxpayer money. It is also charged with finding ways to make government more efficient, ethical, and accountable.

9. What Other Information Sources Will You Use?

Library of Congress - www.loc.gov

The "research arm" of Congress and the largest library in the world.

Smithsonian Institute - www.si.edu

Nineteen museums, nine research centers, and the National Zoo comprise the world's largest museum complex.

10.
HOW DO YOU CONDUCT EFFECTIVE INTERVIEWS?

"Effective interviewing - the practice of getting another person to talk freely - is largely an exercise in human relations."

Edward Jay Friedlander and John Lee - Authors
"Feature Writing for Newspapers & Magazines"

The interview is perhaps the most important writer's tool, leading up to the actual writing of the book. It has the potential to provide both the best and worst information. In-person interviews are best, if possible.

Therefore, the actual art of the interview, is not just the interview itself. It is the aftermath when you determine its credibility, whether it can stand alone, and/or what backup information you might need. Your determination could lead to **additional interviews**.

 Celebrity Interviews

My journalism career has allowed me to interview a number of celebrity notables. They include:

- **Rosa Parks**
- **Walter Cronkite**
- **Smokey Robinson**
- **Congressman John Lewis**
- **Quincy Jones**
- **J.C. Watts (former congressman)**
- **Reverend Joseph Lowery**

I have also had occasion to interview **Travers Bell**, once the sole African American owner of a seat on Wall Street; **Rev. Willie Taplin Barrow**, longtime top aide to Rev. Jesse L. Jackson, Sr.; **Jerry Butler**, former lead singer of the Impressions and member of the Rock & Roll Hall of Fame; **Andrew Brimmer**, former member of the Federal Reserve Board; **Professor Harold Cruse**, the late author of **The Crisis of the Negro Intellectual,** and many other personalities.

My experience has taught me that the bigger they are, the nicer they are. Ego problems, pettiness and other distractions occur, in my view, not with the rich and famous, high and mighty, but, with the small and insignificant.

I have never been disrespected by celebrities. If anything, they have gone out of their way to make me feel comfortable.

Here are a few tips if you happen upon a celebrity interview:

- **Don't be intimidated.**
- **Prepare as usual.**
- **Be prepared for less face time than agreed on.**
- **Be prepared for distractions.**
- **Make sure you clearly communicate your needs to aides.**
- **Don't ask for autographs.**
- **Don't request pictures, except those needed to illustrate.**
- **Be prepared to conduct interview under less than ideal circumstances.**

To the last point, I interviewed Quincy Jones on a crowded elevator, while he was rushing to his limo to catch a flight. I interviewed

10. How Do You Conduct Effective Interviews?

Professor Harold Cruse by phone just before the publication of his long-awaited second book, **Plural But Equal.**

He satisfied himself that I had actually read the book by interviewing me before he would submit to questions. I had quickly read all but the last chapter. I was successful in answering most of his questions.

When I interviewed Smokey Robinson at the Whitehall Hotel in Downtown Chicago, I admitted before the interview that I was a fan who had grown up enjoying his music.

Then I got down to business.

Remember, celebrities breathe in and out just as we do. You will discover that many are so bored with being famous, that they enjoy being treated as regular people.

Whatever the circumstance, you are a professional. Act like one at all times.

Never, ever, submit your finished manuscript to an interviewee. I don't care who they are. If you do, they will review it very carefully and make changes that put themselves in a better light.

Part of what you are seeking in an interview is spontaneity. Plus, you're the professional. Assure subjects that you will contact them if you have further questions, or need clarification about anything that they said.

Oh, I just remembered. I did let one interviewee review my manuscript after it was done and ready for publication.

Who was it?

Walter Cronkite.

Okay, sue me.

In my own defense, I was young, didn't know all of the rules, and was caught off guard.

Plus, at the time in the late 1970s, Walter Cronkite was known as "The most trusted man in America." If you can't trust him, who can you trust?

Look at it this way. I didn't break any rules that I knew of because I was still learning what to do and not do. Still not convinced?

Really, go ahead and sue me.

A. In-person Interviews

If possible, it is always to your advantage to conduct a face-to-face interview with your subject.

Sometimes, scheduling the interview is not possible or convenient. However, meeting the person from whom you are seeking information, gives you several advantages.

Sizing up the prey - If the interview takes place in an interviewee's personal space, what does it look like? Is it well kept, sloppy, or in-between? How does he dress? Is he well kept, sloppy, or in-between? Are books visible in the room?

Family pictures? Wife? Girlfriend? Wife and girlfriend? Children?

How does he treat his staff and other office assistants? Is he polite and professional? Curt and rude?

Does he appear to be organized?

Does he look you straight in the eye? Is he shifty-eyed? Is he hiding something? Truth is he might be. Does he keep looking at his watch? You might have hit on something the subject does not want to discuss or go into great detail about.

Is he courteous? Did he meet you at the agreed upon time?

Does he answer a question with a question? Is he unnecessarily vague? Does he give long-winded answers to simple questions?

The subject might have something to hide.

A good writer is like a good detective. You not only have questions to ask…

But, you must also determine whether you are receiving truthful answers, and to what degree you can use the information.

Scheduling the Interview

When you first identify the subject, call him during business hours to schedule the interview.

Let him know:

- **The subject of the interview**
- **Why you need to interview him**
- **How you discovered his existence**
- **The scope of the interview**
- **How long it will take**
- **Conditions of the interview**

How Long Will It Take?

Unless the interviewee is a personal acquaintance, you should take no more than 30 minutes of his time. Very few people who are worth interviewing will give you more than 30 minutes for an interview, unless they have a personal interest or stake in what you are writing about.

In truth, if you are organized and know what you are doing, you can usually get what you need in 15 to 20 minutes. This includes the obligatory chatting and getting-to-know-you portion of the interview.

Observing personal habits and appearance is important because this knowledge factors into helping you determine the credibility of the interviewee's information. This insight helps facilitate the interview, improving its quality.

For example, a family picture allows you to incorporate, by reference, your family. Golf equipment allows you to talk about your interest in the sport or how you've been intending to learn how to play.

A person's office is a personal portrait of his habits as well as his likes and dislikes. There will be many helpful points of reference in even the most pristine place of business.

Take advantage, but, don't get too personal. You have little time to get the interviewee to like you. However, it doesn't take much time for him to decide he doesn't like you and ban you from his personal space.

During the allotted time, it is essential that you are fast and efficient. In other words, get the information that you need and, then, get out.

Conditions of the Interview

First, unless your subject offers more than the agreed upon time, stick to the agreement. It identifies you as a professional who knows his business and is an efficient practitioner.

However, the reality is that once the subject decides he likes you, that you are competent enough to interview him, he often will give you additional time. If this happens, then make good use of the additional time and stay on point. Don't forget why you scheduled the interview.

Always make every effort to tape the interview. This is important for several reasons.

- **You get an undisputed record of what was said.**
- **You get an undisputed record of the context in which it was said.**
- **It gives easy access to editors, lawyers, or anyone who might need to listen to the tape for legal or other reasons.**

Sometimes people object when they see you preparing to tape the interview. Tell them that the accuracy represented by the recording offers everyone protection.

Once you explain the importance of taping, they usually agree. In 30 or so years of taping interviews, I have never had anyone refuse to be interviewed with the recording after I offered a reasonable explanation.

Let the interviewee know that once you've reviewed your copy, you might need to contact him for a few follow up questions, or clarification of something he said.

Interview Protocol

Before the interview begins, advise the subject that the interview is on the record for publication, if that is the case.

On The Record

By putting the interviewee on notice that the recording is for publication, you are officially ready to begin the interview. That means that anything said is fair game for publication.

Making off-hand comments on the record has gotten many an interview subject in trouble.

Sometimes the comment is made as a joke. Sometimes it is made as a racial, ethnic, religious, sexual orientation, or gender slur. Such language can have unintended consequences.

Sometimes, the off-hand remark is defamatory and can cause real trouble.

Such comments are usually made after the interviewee has decided that he likes you. Not only does he like you, he trusts you.

None of this has anything to do with like or trust.

I repeat, when a person submits to an on-the-record interview, anything he says is fair game for publication.

Once, a married, multi-millionaire businessman confessed to me that his girlfriend and their child live in my home town. His confession took place after I had informed him that we were taping and on the record for publication. Moreover, prior to his confession, he never requested that we move the interview off the record. All I can say is that this gentleman, who confessed his infidelity on the record, got lucky. I was interested in his business and how he became a multi-millionaire. I had no interest in his personal life.

But, he didn't know that.

He was so busy confessing that he failed to realize that I could have chosen to ruin, if not his business life, then certainly his personal life.

I'll say it one more time. Any information transmitted during an on-the-record interview is fair game for publication.

If you see the interview headed in this direction go:

Off The Record

If you are a professional, and not in the confession business, then simply allow the interviewee to go off the record.

I do this when I see the interview getting personal, something that I know the person doesn't want made public. Sometimes the subject will ask to go off the record, when he is having difficulty recalling or explaining information.

Going off the record simply means that you turn off the recording device and stop taking notes. At this point, simply allow the interviewee to talk or silently think through the information until he is comfortable going back on the record and talking for publication.

Once the subject is prepared to go back on the record, restart the recorder and resume taking notes. Start by saying, **"We're now back on the record."** This avoids a later dispute.

Sometimes you encounter a situation when you don't need the interviewee's information for publication; but, you want to inter-view him anyway.

When this happens, you are interviewing the subject for background information only.

Interview For Background Information

Sometimes, you may need to get someone credible to verify information that you already have. You may have received the information from a dubious source or someone whom you believe to be self-serving.

Sometimes, they might even be lying.

You get word that the interviewee can corroborate what you have, but, he doesn't want to be identified as the source.

The easiest way to proceed is to simply show the reluctant interviewee a transcript of what you have and ask him if it is true.

If he verifies the information, simply cite him anonymously in whatever you write, while identifying your named sources. Readers can then draw their own conclusions as to what is true.

The fact that a person can verify information, while seeking anonymity, does not necessarily render him an uncredible source.

People have various reasons for remaining anonymous. They may have happened on the information accidentally. They might be compromised if it were known that they had certain information.

They may have been entrusted with the information by someone else. They may have been somewhere they weren't supposed to be when they came upon the information. They may have stumbled on the information while seeking other information.

The wish to remain unidentified does not necessarily mean that the information is untrue or tainted.

In the **final analysis, you, the writer**, will be charged with determining the truth or falsity of what you are told.

Generally, when people lack an obvious self-interest, or reason to lie, what they say is more likely to be true than not.

B. Telephone Interviews

Most of the advantages you have with an in-person interview disappear when you interview someone by phone.

You can't observe body language, personal surroundings, make eye contact, or take in any other phenomena when you are not in the same room.

But, given the furious pace of today's world, you may as well become comfortable interviewing by phone.

All of the same rules apply as far as on-the-record, off-the-record, and background interviewing.

Phone Interviewing Tips:

- **Advise the subject that you are taping.**
- **Ask the person's patience while you do a sound check.**
- **Have second tape and recorder/digital recording device, in case of malfunction.**
- **Keep questions short and focused.**
- **Have follow up and clarification questions ready.**
- **If you go off the record, then make sure you have the person's voice on recording saying they are ready to go back on the record.**

Caution - Failure to advise a person that he is being recorded may violate federal and state laws.

Federal & State Laws

Federal law allows for recording of telephone conversations, if one party consents. Currently, 38 states and the District of Columbia, generally follow the federal statute.

Before conducting a telephone interview, consult the law that applies in your state and the state you are calling. For example, if you are calling from a one-party consent state to a two-party consent state, **then make sure you have permission from the person whom you are interviewing.**

Currently, twelve states require two-party consent. They are:

California, Connecticut, Florida, Illinois, Maryland, Massachusetts, Michigan, Montana, Nevada, New Hampshire, Pennsylvania and Washington.

* **Illinois' statute** currently requires **two-party** consent. However, case law, developed by both the Illinois Supreme Court and the Illinois appellate courts, has recognized Illinois as a **one-party** state, in cases involving citizens and businesses, not law enforcement.

** **Delaware** presents a challenge because the statute allows "any individual to intercept any wire, oral or electronic communication to which the individual is a party." However, a state privacy law makes it illegal to intercept "without the consent of all parties."

Source: American Legal Guide on Recording Telephone Conversations

 ## C. Online Interviews

Increasingly, you may have occasion to conduct e-mail interviews. When your subject is **Internet** and **Microsoft Word** literate, such interviews can save you both a lot of time.

Plus, you get good information, fast.

A few years ago, I authored an article for a trade journal, updating the status and reliability of electronic voting machines. Even after conducting much traditional research, I was dissatisfied that I could offer any significant new information.

After all, my research was all secondary and I am not an expert.

An expert always lends credibility to you and your subject.

My research did identify Dr. David L. Dill, a Stanford University professor of **Computer Science** and **Electrical Engineering,** who was, and probably remains, the reigning expert on electronic voting machine technology.

Being on deadline, I didn't have a lot of time. I e-mailed him. I continued writing the article, leaving space to drop in his comments in the event he responded. Luckily for me, he did and I conducted a quick online interview.

Once published, that article boosted my reputation as a competent, reliable writer, with demonstrated knowledge of how to use primary, expert sources and timely, secondary sources.

The professor? He gained nothing except the ongoing satisfaction of being known as the expert in his field. He charged nothing and probably spent about 10 minutes sharing his expert information with my audience.

It is also easy to follow up on e-mail interviews and get needed clarification. You also have a permanent record of what was written.

Possibly the greatest advantage to the writer is that you don't have to engage in the time-consuming and sometimes **costly task of transcribing audio.**

10. How Do You Conduct Effective Interviews?

11.
HOW DO YOU WRITE A BOOK PROPOSAL?

"Some writers find it easer to write a book than a proposal. For others, writing the proposal is the most creative part of producing a book."

Michael Larsen - Author
"How To Write A Book Proposal"

Just as a well-developed chapter outline is a blueprint, guiding you, a book proposal documents why a publisher should be interested in your book.

Think of the book proposal as a sales or marketing tool.

It helps you plot your book from beginning to end. It helps determine if there is an audience(s) and, if so, who they are.

Consider the time you spend on your book proposal as important as the time you spend on the book itself. This is the start of the implementation of your publishing plan.

Remember, writing the book is one step. Marketing plus successful publishing, including selecting the right entity to pub-

lish your book helps ensure that it will be bought, read, and discussed.

At the point you decide to write a book, you should begin researching the marketing and publishing process. Too many people write books, good books, that nobody knows exist.

If your book's existence is unknown, no one will buy it, and you might as well have spent your time engaged in some other activity.

A. Short Proposal

Many publishers have their own proposal guidelines, which you must follow without variation. The slightest departure from the publisher's stated guidelines spells failure. This is especially true in the case of your major publishers like Henry Holt, Time Books, Random House, and others. Do exactly what they request.

This is also true when preparing your manuscript.

You will see variations on the following format, when reading other books on this subject. Different authors emphasize different things.

Some publishers offer informal guidelines. This is information they expect to see in any proposal. Do not send a proposal to a publisher who **does not accept unsolicited material.**

In the absence of guidelines, most publishers expect to see at least the following:

1. **Brief Description** - Describe what you intend to write about as concisely as possible.

2. **Why This Book is Necessary** - This section is especially important if you are writing about a popular subject, which has already been covered many times, by many people. Some of these people are better known than you and are experts in the field. **What can you offer that's not already known?**

Similar Books Already Published - A brief review of books previously published on the subject shows that you are not naive. It shows awareness that the subject has been covered by different authors. Some come with different points of view. Others may have superior writing skills, experience, and professional credentials.

3. **Outstanding Features** - Discuss how your book is different from the competition. Your effort may be as simple as an update on previously published information. If you are writing about the technology field, your book may update the latest technology, or product. **You're seeking a different hook here.** Few subjects worth writing about have been entirely exhausted.

4. **Format & Structure** - Is it written chronologically? Reverse chronological order? Does it jump in and out of different time frames? **Format and structure** will depend in part on your subject. If you're writing an updated history of past presidents, it's likely to be chronological. Although it could easily begin with the current president.

   If you're writing a thriller, or murder mystery, then it might, for effect, start with the death of a main character or the trial of the accused and work its way back. Your **chapter description** will greatly assist you in developing this section.

5. **Primary Audience(s)** - You are writing for an audience. Sometimes your audience is obvious. If you're updating a textbook on Constitutional Law, then students and teachers are obviously your intended targets. Often, you are targeting multiple audiences with overlapping interests.

   Librarians, bookstore managers, and others who make buying decisions are included as target audiences for this book. Make sure to identify at least three targeted primary audiences.

6. **Secondary Audience(s)** - All others are secondary. Several years ago I worked with **R&B singer** and **Rock & Roll Hall of**

Famer, Jerry Butler on his autobiography.

When I submitted my book proposal to the music acquisitions editor at the University of Illinois Press, I identified the following audiences.

Primary

- Researchers interested in this music
- Students of music history
- General & Special Interest Librarians
- Anyone interested in the business of music
- African American women ages 30 and up
- African American men ages 30 and up

Secondary

- Other American ethnic groups who like the R&B and Easy Listening formats
- African American teens and young adults
- Other ethnic youth groups
- International markets including Caribbean, Africa, and other 3rd World countries

Later in my research, I discovered that Butler was popular with what is called the *"Beach Music"* scene, which includes white teenagers on spring beach breaks. I added this information in subsequent proposals.

7. **Primary Sources** - Where are you going to get your information? Primary sources give you first-hand information. If you are writing a biography, or autobiography, **primary sources would include:**
   - Friends and family of the subject
   - People who worked with subject
   - People who taught and mentored the subject
   - Others who have unfiltered, first-hand knowledge of the subject
   - Certain types of documents and reference materials

8. **Chapter Description (Outline)** - The chapter description is a one or two paragraph depiction of each chapter. It is a very important section of the proposal because it is the longest, most descriptive look at your proposed book to a prospective publisher.

9. **Author's Qualifications** - The author's qualification component of the book proposal presents an unnecessary challenge for most first-timers. If you've never written for publication, then don't dwell on it. Pull on your collective writing experience, whether it was a formal research paper or an article that made your school newspaper.

   Remember, if your published-writing experience is limited, a publisher may only have the quality of your written proposal to evaluate.

   When you reflect, everyone has written something. Anything that demonstrates your skill and talent as a writer is on the table.

   Don't overplay your lack of experience. Don't embellish what you haven't done. It will appear that you lack confidence, or worse, that you are dishonest. Your experience, or lack thereof, is what it is.

   Your proposal and cover letter will be your first and, possibly, last chance to impress potential publishers that you can write.

   Be honest. Write right, with no typos or grammatical mishaps. Write clearly and passionately. Your first chance to get published could be your last.

10. **Conclusion** - Be brief and tie up loose ends. Don't beg or whine. Show confidence. Maintain a positive attitude that demonstrates your intention to get **published**, whatever it takes.

B. Academic Proposal

Due to limited budgets, most academic presses are limited in what they can publish. They are also limited in subject matter and very specific about their academic interests.

The **ASSOCIATION OF AMERICAN UNIVERSITY PRESSES DIRECTORY (AAUP)** is an important reference that lists all major university presses in the country. Published by the **University of Chicago Press**, www.press.uchicago.edu; this is an essential source documenting the interests of the various university presses.

No matter the academic subject you are pursuing, if it's important to scholars, then one of these presses will have an interest. If you don't find your area of interest, then you might want to rethink its relevance.

However, before you move on, make sure it's not a cutting edge topic that academia hasn't yet discovered.

As an introduction and guide to the world of university presses, the **AAUP DIRECTORY** is an important reference and resource for anyone wanting to be involved in scholarly publishing.

Its many useful features include detailed entries for each member press and guidelines for submitting manuscripts.

Following are random references to three large and three small university presses. This vividly illustrates the variety of subject matter interests.

Large University Presses

1. **Cornell University Press** - Serious nonfiction with titles ranging from Asian Studies, Politics and International Relations to Veterinary Science.

2. **Duke University Press** - Scholarly books in Humanities and Social Science. Interests in Gay and Lesbian Studies, American Studies and African American Studies.

3. University of Illinois Press - Interests in scholarly books and serious non-fiction. Titles range from Music to Archaeology to Native American Studies.

Small University Presses

1. Georgetown University Press - Interests include Language and Linguistics, International Affairs and Public Policy.

2. Howard University Press - Interested in serious non-fiction and any area of scholarship. Focus includes African American Studies, Communications, History, Literature, and Social Science.

3. University of New Mexico - Interested in scholarly books and serious non-fiction. Titles range from History of Photography, Natural History, Western American Literature and Latin American History.

Source: AAUP Directory - See latest edition available. Lists over 100 university press operations; including contact information; names of acquisitions editors and their specialties; and other important information for those interested in this type of writing. Visit www.aaupnet.org.

Once you have determined that a specific press publishes your book's subject matter, then identify the appropriate acquisitions editor for future reference and contact.

When your proposal is ready, this person will be a primary, if not *the* primary, point of contact. If you have questions or need clarification as you develop your proposal, then the acquisitions editor or designee is the person to contact.

Do not become a nuisance. Make sure you need editorial input before you make contact. You don't want to make a negative impression before the press even receives your proposal.

A typical academic proposal contains the following:

1. A cover letter, describing the length of the manuscript (number of words or number of double-spaced pages), and any intended elements other than text, such as photographs, musical scores, graphs, line drawings, or tables; also, if the manuscript is not yet finished, then let the university press know when you expect to finish.

2. A table of contents

3. One or two sample chapters that accurately reflect the nature and quality of your work

4. A copy of your resume or curriculum vitae

5. The names of any experts who have already read your manuscript or are familiar with your work

Excerpt from University of Illinois Press Submission Guidelines:

Proposals are generally evaluated within three weeks of receipt. You should feel free to submit your proposal to as many presses as you wish, but please inform us if you have done so.

Also, we prefer to receive proposals first, unsolicited manuscripts will be considered for publication, though it may take longer for us to reach a decision.

What is meant, but not said here is, "Just send us a proposal. We can tell after reviewing whether it is worth your time, or ours, to go any further."

Take note that other university presses may not be as liberal, preferring not to spend precious staff time weighing through what may turn out to be an unpublishable manuscript.

Sometimes, university press guidelines offer suggestions on dos and don'ts. If there are none, then let common sense guide you. If you are unsure whether they accept exclusive submissions only,…ask.

When an academic press has special requirements, they will let you know. For example, the University of Chicago Press requires proposals to be mailed, not faxed or e-mailed.

More from the University of Illinois Press Submission Guidelines:

A well-written manuscript can enter the publication stream in as little as three to four months from the date of initial submission, though much depends on the co-operation of referees and your willingness to make necessary revisions in a timely manner.

If extensive revisions are called for, the time frame expands according to your professional and personal commitments and the availability of one or more of the referees to evaluate the revised manuscript.

Understand that your manuscript will not make it to a referee, or anyone else, if it has not favorably impressed an internal acquisitions editor.

It cannot be stressed enough that your initial submission should be as well-written and professionally prepared as possible.

In this game, a bad first impression may be your last chance to impress.

If you are seriously intent on producing an academic book, **Getting It Published,** by William Germano, comes highly recommended. This guide is the most thorough, easily accessible reference you are likely to find on the subject.

What do Publishers Do? - Excerpt from *Getting It Published*

Publishers select books for several reasons.

- The book will make a lot of money and appeal to many readers.

- The book will only make a small amount of money, but it requires little investment and involves small risk because it fits with other titles on the list and is easy to promote.

- The book is by an author whose presence on the list will enhance the publisher's reputation and increase the house's attractiveness to other authors and agents, some of whose projects will make the house a lot of money.

- The book is by an author who is already on the publisher's list and whose loyalty will be rewarded.

- The book comes highly recommended by someone on whom the publisher in some way depends.

- The book, flawed or not, is great.

Much of what Germano says here could apply to any type of book, not just academic.

Germano continues, *"At a scholarly house, there are other, more particular reasons for selecting books. Academic prestige is one. Is the book so strong that it will win awards by scholarly associations? For some houses, this is a distinct and important reason to take a project on."* Publishers also consider whether a book will have a long shelf life, resulting in continuous sales over a long period of time.

A Note on Manuscript Preparation

If you want your book to be published by a reputable publisher, then it is highly recommended that you first submit a proposal following all of the publisher's suggested guidelines, rather than submitting a completed manuscript.

However, despite my best advice, I know that many of you feel so strongly about your book project that you are going to plow ahead and produce a "publishable" manuscript.

Before doing so, consult www.writecontent.com/Publishing for an excellent guide to proper manuscript preparation. Although there are many other good sources available both online and offline, this is one that I highly recommend.

11. How Do You Write A Book Proposal?

12.
WHO WILL PUBLISH YOUR BOOK?

*"No writer likes not to be edited,
as much as he dislikes not to be published."*

Russell Lynes

Who will publish your book may depend on:

- **How Much Control You Want**
- **Book Subject**
- **Resources**
- **Timing Of Book**

How much Control Do You Want?

Some people decide to write a book because they think it will give them the financial and artistic freedom over their lives that they've always craved.

They view the process as solitary and one that allows them to exercise complete control.

That's true to a certain point.

The crafting of a book is indeed a time of enforced solitary.

Even as I write this it's a nice, sunny day in Chicago. I would much rather be sitting on the lakefront or the riverfront eating a Klondike Bar and watching rich people sail their boats.

But here I sit.

What you should absolutely understand is, **from now on**, this is no longer a solitary process.

By now, you should be considering who will publish your book. There are various options; some are more costly and time-consuming than others. Self-publishing is always an option, depending on your interests and circumstances.

Very shortly, I will discuss the various professionals you will need to engage to get your book to the market.

Book Subject

The subject of your book will help determine who should publish your book.

Some publishing companies simply do not publish certain types of books, no matter how well-written, timely, or well intentioned.

Resources - See Chapter 17 - MONEY, WHO NEEDS IT? YOU DO IF YOU WRITE A BOOK

Timing Of Book

Spring, just before the summer vacation season, and leading up to the Christmas buying season are the prime times for book publishing companies.

If your book revolves around a holiday or a season, then you must know when buyers make their decisions in order to ensure the product arrives in time to retail outlets to greet customers and their check books, debit and credit cards.

This remains a consideration, although online purchases are increasingly taking over a larger part of the book sales market.

Once your proposal is accepted, determine when the publisher needs a finished copy shipped to bookstores.

Ask what steps are involved and how long it will take.

There are two major upsides to having your book released during one of these two peak times:

> **A. People often have disposable income.**
> **B. People are actively seeking gifts for themselves and others.**

The downside? You face more competition. Therefore, it's on you to produce a well-written, eye-catching product that is the beneficiary of a deftly executed marketing campaign.

Publishing your book during these times also means:

> **A. You must satisfy a unique market niche.**
> **B. Your book must withstand extra scrutiny to ensure success.**

Having said all of that, let's review your basic publishing options.

A. Mainstream Large Press

We would all like our books to be embraced and published by a major house like **Random House, Ballantine Books,** or **Harper Collins**, especially our first time out.

Your chances of this happening are slim and slimmer, especially if you are an unknown first-timer. If it happens, expect to give up a great deal of artistic control and more.

Once a major publisher signs you, they own you and your book, subject to the stipulations in the contract, which, except in highly unusual circumstances, will be their standard contract.

Any money received up front will be charged against later royalties you might receive.

In the unlikely event you get signed by a major publisher, your first time out, you will have no problem finding an agent.

In fact, once you are notified by a major publisher of their interest in discussing a contract, find an agent. A good agent knows how to negotiate fine points to your advantage.

As mentioned in a later chapter, reputable agents typically do not sully themselves with unknown, first-time authors.

However, if a major publisher shows interest, immediately begin interviewing agents.

Prepare to yield control. What do you get in return?

   A. An advance, maybe
   B. A well-executed marketing plan
   C. Other support to help sell your book
   D. An able editor to improve your work

And, if the publisher wants to change plot lines, characters, direction and the overall tone of your book, the standard contract probably allows them to do so.

Why would you sign such a document?

Simple, you would sign such a document in order to get your book published by a major company and then do the big time talk-show circuit.

B. Small Press/Imprints

This prospect is more likely. These presses have fewer resources, so you give up less. However, keep in mind that **Imprints** are owned by major publishing houses in order to publish niche publications for targeted audiences.

Depending on their operational relationship with their parent, they may have more resources than the typical small press operation.

Remember, all presses, large or small, are in business to make money.

C. Alternative/Specialty/Ethnic Press

If you are interested in these categories, then there are numerous directories and other information, online and print, that will give you what you need.

D. University Press

See Chapter 11 B. Academic Proposals Discussed.

E. Self-Publishing

This has become increasingly popular, especially for first-time authors. See Resource Guide for more information.

A Note About The Vanity Press

If you choose this option, then you are literally paying to have your book published. This is often, but should not be, confused with **Self-Publishing** where you retain the right to make significant decisions about your manuscript, while also incurring out-of-pocket costs.

Vanity Press is listed simply as another option to consider. See www.VanityPress.com, as an example of a Vanity Press publisher.

13.

WHAT NOW?

"A man will turn over half a library to make one book."

James Boswell - Author

As you get closer to finishing your book, remember the first draft will not be ready to go to press no matter which publishing option you choose.

While completion of the first draft is a good place to be, it's just that, a first draft. As you were crafting this draft, you should have already begun proofreading and copy editing.

Proofread and edit your draft periodically. Otherwise, the finished first draft will not be a seamless read.

If, for the most part, your first draft makes sense to you, then you are ready to move forward.

It's now time to begin thinking about:

A. **Registering your Copyright - For more detail on the copyright issue, See Chapter 19 - What Do You Need To Know About The Law?** What is important to know right now is that your work receives copyright protection as soon as it is produced. Registration is important in case there is ever a dispute over who owns the copyright.

   Go to www.copyright.gov for all you need to know about the copyright registration process.

B. **Applying for an ISBN** - Formerly a 10-digit number, the **International Standard Book Number**, better known as **ISBN**, is now 13-digits. This number is important because it uniquely identifies your book, separating it from all others, published and yet-to-be published. It is a unique **marketing tool** that facilitates sales with major wholesalers and retailers.

   Go to www.isbn.org for all you need to know about how to secure an **ISBN**.

C. **Securing a Bar Code** - Remember, you must secure your **ISBN** before obtaining a **Bar Code**. Again, most major retailers and wholesalers require a Bar Code, which allows the **ISBN,** and other information unique to the book, to be easily scanned. If your intent is to sell a lot of books, use the **Bookland EAN Bar Code**, which incorporates the **ISBN** and is identified by a **978** prefix, the first three digits of the 13 number **ISBN**.

   Readers may be more familiar with the **UPC Bar Code (United Product Code)**. If you commonly purchase books from department stores, drug stores, or other retail outlets, that carry merchandise, other than books, you are likely to see the **UPC** affixed to your copy.

   Go to www.bowkerbarcode.com for all you need to know about the cost of **Bar Codes** and how to secure them.

D. Applying for the LCCN (Library of Congress Control Number) - If you want your book to reside within a library, then apply for a **LCCN**. This is a unique number assigned by the Library of Congress. It allows libraries to track your book in whatever bibliographic system they use, most likely an online automated format.

Go to www.loc.gov for all you need to know about securing an LCCN.

It is also time to start thinking about identifying:

A. Additional Readers (for initial feedback)
B. Proofreader(s)
C. Copy Editor
D. Attorney

Before doing so, carefully review all copy at least twice. Make sure that it:

A. Says what you want to say
B. Says it the right way
C. Is cliché and jargon free
D. Is in the proper sequence
E. Withstands legal scrutiny
F. Is factually correct

ADDITIONAL READERS

After carefully reviewing all copy at least twice, turn it over to a couple of friends or family members whose skill and judgment you trust. It's important to select people who will give you honest feedback, not those who will trip over themselves to make you feel good.

Instruct them to read objectively, as if they don't know you. Ask them to be honest when giving feedback. Let them know why you need their honest input, explaining that it is important in helping you improve the final copy.

When they are done, review their comments, and ask them for clarification, where necessary.

Finally, ask them if they would buy the book and why. If they say they wouldn't buy it, even if their first born's life was at stake, then ask how you can change their minds.

PROOFREADER(S)

After incorporating revisions, identify a proofreader, preferably a professional. Understand that proofreading is different from copy editing, which will be discussed shortly.

A proofreader will make corrections and changes to your copy. They will correct typos and grammatical errors. They are unlikely to suggest reworking, or make wholesale revisions to your copy.

COPY EDITOR(S)

Judith Appelbaum, author of the highly recommended, *How To Get Happily Published* points out the crucial **difference in proofreading** and **copy editing**.

"To Copy-edit is to be responsible for making a manuscript correct in all its details."

Appelbaum contends that it is the copy editor's responsibility to demand documentation of authenticity from the author.

She writes, *"More and more documentation is the author's job because fewer and fewer publishers can afford to have a fact checker on the staff nowadays."*

ATTORNEY

Even after all of those eyes have reviewed and commented on your copy, let an attorney, preferably a First Amendment specialist, give it a good once over.

13. What Now?

The lawyer should carefully review the copy to ensure that it is **defamatory free** and has not violated **copyright** and **fair use** laws.

See discussion of **legal issues in Chapter 19** for a more complete explanation of **copyright and the doctrine of fair use**. It is recommended that you seek author's permission for use of all **copyrighted material** because fair use laws are extremely vague.

If you can't get written permission, then leave that particular information out. You do not need a law suit at this point in your career.

Who Will Distribute Your Book?

You are now ready to consider what outlets might distribute your book, once it is published.

Typically, first-time authors consider the following distribution outlets:

A. **Mainstream bookstores**
B. **Alternative bookstores**
C. **Retail outlets**
D. **Specialty stores**
E. **Ethnic bookstores**
F. **School bookstores**
G. **Libraries**

Online Distribution Sources

- **Alternative Press Center - www.altpress.org - a not-for-profit advocate that increases awareness of the Alternative Press industry**
- **Amazon.com**
- **Barnes and Noble**
- **Booksprice.com**
- **Greenleaf Book Group - www.greenleafbookgroup.com - a premier distributor serving the independent self-publisher and small press markets**
- **Independent Publishers Group - www.ipgbooks.com**

- Ingram Distribution Group, Inc. - www.ingrambooks. com - largest wholesaler distributor to independent bookstores
- Quality Books Inc. - www.qbi-com - major distributor to libraries

OTHER

Also know that, depending on the book's subject and the audiences you might be seeking, there is a whole category of additional distribution opportunities, broadly categorized as *other*.

Suppose your book is about **Youth Financial Literacy.** In addition to some of the more obvious distribution possibilities, consider using the following kiosks, or other outlets as available:

A. Outdoor festivals
B. Parks
C. Children's retail outlets
D. Museums
E. Amusement parks
F. Zoos
G. Child and family-friendly restaurants
H. Airport gift shops

There are others, but the above list gives you a good start at identifying additional outlets for your book.

13. What Now?

14.
WHAT PROFESSIONAL HELP DO YOU NEED?

"Nothing is particularly hard if you divide it into small jobs."

Henry Ford

It takes more than just your time.

When you set out to write a book, there comes a time when you must engage other experts to get it on the street as well as into bookstores, libraries, and readers' hands.

For me, that time has come.

I am starting to visualize how the finished product will look; how many copies I will need; how many pages; what kind of paper; what kind of cover and interior design? What will be the final title? Make sure it's catchy.

How much color?

Other questions have popped into my head. How will I publicize my book? Who, how and when will the marketing take place? When and how will it be distributed? How do I get it placed in bookstores so it will be seen? What other types of distribution should I consider?

These are just some of the questions I am currently considering. Others will emerge as I continue.

A. GRAPHIC DESIGNER

Think about the last time you bought a book. Think of the last time you looked for a book. Did you know what you were looking for? Fiction, non-fiction, murder mystery, romance, comedy, true crime, or other? You weren't sure. You were just looking.

What finally caught your attention? Was it a color, or combination of colors? Title? Subject? Display design? A combination of factors?

The title and cover design are the two most important factors in helping a potential buyer decide to pick up and review your book. If you get someone to that point, hopefully they will read the liner notes on the back.

If they still haven't tossed it aside, and actually open it to glance at the testimonials and introduction, you just might have a sale.

I can't emphasize enough the importance of your cover design. Once someone picks your book up and takes a closer look, you're a step closer to that all important cha ching.

So, take your time in carefully selecting the right graphic designer. Many designers have samples of their work online, enabling you to do careful reviews on your own time.

Once you have reviewed several designers, contact them. Give them the book's specifications and invite them to bid for the work. Make sure you give them all the same specs. That's the only way you will be able to compare the bids.

Typically, expect to receive one bid that is way high, and one that is way low. Often the lower than expected bid is by someone with little experience; but one who may have just the right amount of talent and temperament that you are looking for.

I do not recommend that you make your selection based solely on the cost. That could be a big mistake.

When you interview designers, or any other creative talent, make sure they are even-tempered and easy to work with. The worse thing for you, and your book project, is to find out too late that you have signed on a talented egomaniac.

Trust me, some of them are as crazy as they are talented.

Fortunately, there are enough in the talent pool to enable you to find one who fits your professional needs.

The person submitting the highest bid is not necessarily the most talented. Also, there are some very talented young people out there who make up in skills what they lack in experience.

Once signed, designers will want a quarter to a third retainer up front, with the rest paid at various stages, including completion of the project. Most, with whom I've worked, will allow up to three revisions without extra charges.

It's highly recommended, and more cost-effective, if you use the same graphic designer for the cover and interior design of your book.

B. PRINTER

Once you have selected a graphic designer, one of the first conversations you should have is about selecting a printer. Most graphic designers have preferred printers with whom they have worked.

This arrangement gives you several benefits because it enables the designer to interface with the printer. They speak the same technical language, which is an advantage they have that you don't.

So, even if the graphic designer's preferred printer costs a little more, go for it. First, it makes the designer happy. A happy designer makes for a better designed book. If you force feed a printer to the designer just to save a few bucks, I guarantee you'll be sorry.

In addition, you will have caused the designer to lose out on the 10 to 15 percent administrative fee that they often fold into their estimate. If it's not part of the designer's estimate, then the printer typically works it into his fee. This probably won't be discussed with you, until a good, professional working relationship has been developed. Designers' and printers' explanations about the purpose of a fee will vary.

My best guesstimate is that designers include an administrative fee as their cost for working with the printer. I believe that printers include an administrative fee as a hedge against any overruns and to protect them against underestimating the costs of the work.

The reason the administrative fee is usually not discussed is obvious. Graphic designers and printers want to make you feel that they are giving you their best estimate. They know you may have concerns about what you might consider a surcharge, especially if you are unfamiliar with the design and printing process.

Don't look on this fee as a kickback. It is likely to be well-earned. When production problems arise, you can go directly to the graphic designer. They then can express the problem, in necessary technical language, to the printer.

When you have reviewed and revised all of the designer's proofs, copy then goes to the printer. Make sure your contract requires the printer to do a proof before submitting final copy.

14. What Professional Help Do You Need?

Caution - Any changes you make at this stage of the production can be very costly. This is where you usually find out that estimates are just that. Estimates rarely reflect what you end up paying to both the graphic designer and printer.

Therefore, make sure you have two to three excellent, and preferably paid, proofreaders and copy editors review copy before it goes to the printer. The money is well spent because you get a better final copy and will pay out less to the printer in the end.

No matter how many printed copies you order, there are likely to be overruns or underruns. If an overrun, those extra copies belong to you at no extra cost. Make sure you have a line item in your contract specifying this. To protect against an underrun, ensure that your contract says how many you are having printed.

Ask about the overrun once the job is done. If you don't and the job turns out well, the printer is likely to take the extra copies for his own use in marketing his company.

Printers grow their operations with repeat business and word of mouth. That's not likely to happen if customers are unsatisfied.

C. LAWYER

As much as you love to hate them, hire a lawyer to help guide you through what can be a very complex process. If you've done everything right, then you will mostly need your lawyer to draft contracts and review copy, not to defend you in court.

You should have written contracts for your graphic designer and printer. Hopefully, one contract will suffice, especially if the printer sub-contracts with the designer.

If you retain a publicist or public relations firm, draft a contract. Fees and duties should be explicitly listed.

Caveat - You should have a contract drafted for any professional whom you employ to produce, publish, market and distribute your book.

In the unfortunate event you get sued or go to court for any reason, don't go by yourself, take your lawyer.

In the beginning you might hire an attorney to carry out specific tasks. If you begin making a lot of money, and this turns into a career, then it might be time to permanently retain an attorney or firm.

D. ACCOUNTANT/BUSINESS MANAGER

You want to spend your waking hours writing, not shuffling papers. Hire someone who can:

- Keep track of the paperwork
- Set up tax files
- Find receipts at tax time
- Maintain an efficient business
- Answer business-related questions
- Help you expand when the time comes

Caveat - You should be in charge of your business at all times. That means:

- Knowing where files are kept
- Being able to answer business-related questions, when necessary
- Knowing the status of all of your projects
- Being on top of everything

E. PUBLICIST

The worst waste of your time is writing a book that no one reads. What might be the main reason?

No one knows it exists.

Caveat - Word of mouth is never enough. If you don't know how to publicize your book, hire someone who can.

Trust me, in this economy there are skilled publicists, public relations people, promotional experts, Internet marketing specialists, and others just waiting on your call.

But you won't call them because you don't know that they exist.

14. What Professional Help Do You Need?

That means that it is past time for you to begin networking in order to find the right people you need to help you publicize your book.

Want to get it reviewed? There are people who can help you.

Want your book title and name to surface at the top of a Google search? There are people who can help you.

Want to hit the speaker's circuit to promote your book? There are people who can help you.

Want to hit the local and national radio airwaves to discuss your book? There are people who can help you.

Want to get on television, get your book into the library, get a display at a publisher's trade show, and get promoted by social media outlets? Yes, there are people who can help you.

Caveat - Make sure that whomever you retain to help promote your book has the necessary contacts, media and other, and technological expertise. One good person and his network should be all you need to get the word out.

There will be more about marketing, distribution, and promotion in later chapters and in the **Best Resource Guide.**

15.

DO YOU NEED AN AGENT?

*"You don't need one until you're making enough for someone to steal...
and if you're making that much, you're making enough
to take your pick of good agents."*

Stephen King's first rule of writers and agents.

The short answer is no, you do not need an agent

The agent willing to represent an unknown, unpublished, untested writer is probably the agent you don't want, except if you happen to attract the interest of a major publisher your first time around the track.

But then again, in this economy, who knows? This economy is so upside down, I can't say that you won't walk out of your door in the next 20 minutes and see an A-list agent wearing a sandwich sign reading, **"Will represent first time author for food."**

This is especially true if you live in an area like New York or Chicago, which are both major publishing centers.

Hopefully, after this painful economy passes, things will return to normal.

Normal means that A-list agents seek out A-list clients. Unless your work has received an unusual amount of advance publicity and favorable reviews, it is unlikely that any good agent, worth the top dollar he usually commands, is going to try to find you.

If you're like the majority of first-timers, you'd better prepare to go it alone. That means learning as much as you can about the book publishing industry and your options.

Even if you retain an agent, educate yourself about the publishing industry to avoid becoming a broke, unwitting dupe. You can burn a lot of Benjamins trying to get published if you don't know what you're doing.

15. Do You Need An Agent?

16.
HOW WILL YOU
MARKET YOUR BOOK?

*"It will always be up to you to provide the motivation
for readers to buy your books."*

*John Kremer - Author
"1001 Ways to Market Your Books"*

You've finished, or almost completed, your first book. You should feel good. This is a major step.

But, it's just the beginning.

Say what?

Yes, writing your book doesn't mean a thing if you don't implement an effective marketing plan, one that makes full use of today's awesome technology.

Effective marketing of, what I assume is, a well-written book, is what will ring up the cha ching and make all of your efforts worthwhile.

If I had come clean with you earlier, you might not have written your book.

Since you took that time-consuming first step, what now?

Only you can decide whether you need to engage a professional to create and implement your plan. There is such an abundance of good information available, I recommend you first do your own research to determine what basic tools you need to get started.

Once done, you might want to talk to a couple of professionals to get their thoughts as well as information on their experience, track records, and fees.

Once you have a good idea of what needs to be done, then it's time to decide whether you have the time and/or skill to give your book the marketing plan it deserves.

Choosing A Professional

You're in luck. Thanks to the ongoing recession/depression, it's a buyer's market. You won't have any trouble finding a good-to-great marketing person. They are all over the place.

Take your time choosing a professional marketer who is tailor-made to give your book the proper care and feeding it requires, just like a newborn.

When choosing your marketing person, consider the following:

- **Passion**
- **Ethics**
- **Honesty**
- **References**
- **Talent**
- **Contacts**
- **Listening skills**
- **Aggressiveness**
- **Verified track record**
- **Punctuality**

Passion, Ethics & Honesty

Why, you might ask, do I insist on passion, ethics and honesty before talent?

It is simple. Talent is easier to find.

A talented marketing professional who lacks passion about your project, a personal code of ethics, and a commitment to day-to-day honesty, is a woeful waste of your time and cash. This type of individual could even harm your reputation.

You do not want to be just another client.

Interview and consider at least two people or firms. This will give you a basis for comparison. Check and evaluate references after the interview, if you are interested.

Before you make a decision, remember that no one is perfect.

If someone appears perfect, then make sure the references are not relatives, good friends, or creditors trying to get paid.

Make sure the references are credible. Once you sign a contract, you're stuck for the length of the agreement.

Signing A Contract

Make the first contract short, either project specific, or for a definite time. Select a fee structure that works for you.

Typical agreements include:

- One-third or one-fourth retainer, remainder at designated intervals, final on satisfactory completion
- Payment per project
- Hourly agreement

Hourly agreements can present a problem for you. That's why honesty and ethics are so important. It is very easy for the marketer to tack on an hour here, an hour there, for work they may not have performed.

Your worse case scenario is getting into a fee argument with your marketing professional. They can jam you 1,000 different ways.

Make that 1,001, I just thought of another way.

I recommend agreeing on a specific price for a project. Include the estimated number of hours to complete the project. Include a contract clause that specifies what is to be paid and the rate to be paid.

Determine first, who is at fault and, then, go from there.

If you go the hourly rate, once again, project how many hours for which you will be billed and the rate. This, again, covers you if the project goes over budget.

If All Else Fails...

Sometimes the best intended agreements fail. Try to avoid small claims court or other litigation by agreeing to **contract mediation.** Include a cancellation or opt-out clause. Sixty days written is typical, but you decide the terms.

If this fails, take the sucker to court. It probably won't be the first, or last, time.

A. **Traditional Marketing** - The best strategic marketing plan for your book will blend **Traditional Marketing** and **Online Marketing,** which now includes the latest technological phenomena, **Social Media Marketing**.

Whether your book is produced by a publishing company, or you decide to self-publish, be prepared to take the lead in marketing your book.

16. How Are You Going To Market Your Book?

Who cares about it more than you?

John Kremer, in *1001 Ways to Market Your Books*, suggests five promotional activities a day.

Promotional Activities can include:
- Sending out press materials
- Scheduling a media appearance
- Updating website
- Setting up a speaking engagement
- Talking to potential wholesalers

Even if a reputable publisher has pegged your book as a likely winner, they must still spread limited resources in many directions. Most authors will only try to promote one book at a time. That is, unless your name is **James Patterson**.

One of the first and most essential promotional pieces you need to develop is a **media kit**, also known as a **press kit**. You will need a hard copy and electronic version.

The hard copy is best displayed in a two-pocket folder. Some prefer tiered inserts for effect because only the heading is displayed when opened. This type of package is **cost-effective** because it allows the replacement of dated information, without reproducing the whole kit.

A typical **media kit** includes:
- Review copy of book
- Book-related press release
- Author's bio
- Professional, glossy 8X10 author photo
- Book fact sheet
- Copies of previous reviews and testimonials

Some publishers and authors include book-related promos, calendars, bookmarks, key chains, and the like.

I recommend that a cover letter, also called a pitch letter, be tailored to whomever you are sending the information. People have different reactions to form letters, not always favorable.

You must become media savvy because your efforts will be directed toward obtaining:

- Publication exposure
- Radio and television exposure
- Internet exposure
- Special event exposure

Your marketing efforts should also focus on:

- Educational institutions
- Events targeting writers and publishers
- Special events
- Book clubs
- Other venues
- Other events related to the subject matter of your book

There are other activities you can do to create buzz about your book. Start a newsletter. Review other books for a local publication. Start a book-related talk show on your local cable outlet.

Nothing inspires people more to search for your book than hearing your name and the title of the book mentioned repeatedly in different settings.

My purpose here is not to make you a marketing expert. It is to inform you of the importance of developing and executing a sound marketing plan.

You don't have to be an expert to plan and execute. You do need to know that effective marketing dictates the success of your book.

As I indicated earlier, you may need to hire an expert. If you do, you still need to know enough about what they are doing to offer input.

After all, it is your book.

Only you can decide whether your precious time is better spent doing it yourself or if it's better to spend money on a pro.

Either way, you must educate yourself about the process. For some reason, people often think they can cut corners when it comes to marketing. This belief is **part ego** and **part stupidity.**

There is also the false notion that anyone, trained or not, can develop and execute a successful marketing program.

I once overhead a woman loudly proclaim to her husband in a mall; *"You're not only wrong, you couldn't be more wrong."*

And, so it is with the business of marketing. It does take someone who knows what they are doing to produce an effective marketing strategy.

After all, it is your book.

If you've decided that you don't have money in the budget and that you have more passion and energy than know-how, then, what follows are three of the best references on the subject:

1. *Dan Poynter's Self-Publishing Manual*
2. *1001 Ways to Market Your Books*
3. *Self Publishing for Dummies*

B. Online Marketing

Not long ago, developing an **Online Marketing** plan for your book would have been limited to:

1. **Website**
2. **E-mail**
3. **Chat rooms**
4. **Blog**

Not anymore.

If, like many, you have longed for the Internet to simply disappear and leave you alone…

Fuhgetaboutit

That train has long ago left the station. It's not by accident that you are standing on the platform, virtually alone.

Do not, I repeat, do not limit your efforts to traditional marketing. Also, don't over-rely on your marketing expert, if you choose to hire one.

At the very least:
- **Develop a website.**
- **Create a blog and keep it updated.**
- **Determine which Social Media outlets to access.**
- **Determine how to incorporate Social Media into your marketing plan.**
- **Take advantage of invitations to join existing Social Media networks, where appropriate.**

What is Social Media Marketing?

"Social media marketing is an engagement with online communities to generate exposure, opportunity and sales."

Wikipedia - Online Encyclopedia

Also known as Social Marketing, Online Marketing, and other terms that mean the same thing. This phenomena is a cost-effective way to locate the greatest number of people who:

Are interested in your book

The most effective use of these online tools enable you to reach the people who can:

Reach others who are interested in your book

According to Dana Lynn Smith, author of ***The Savvy Book Marketer's Guide To Successful Social Marketing***, *this type of* **"user endorsement** *is more effective than* **traditional marketing."**

Caution - Do not try to implement every suggestion or tip that you encounter on the Internet and elsewhere.

There is so much available that you might become over-whelmed.

If you had to describe marketing in one word, think of the word **STRATEGIC**. Your plan must be strategic to be effective.

If your plan does not create more buzz and demand for your book, then it is ineffective; it is not strategic.

Therefore, even before you learn what's available to you... before you learn anything about **Social Media Marketing**, think about:

- Why did you write your book?
- For whom did you write your book?
- Where can you find these people in Cyberspace?
- How do you uniquely identify or brand you and your book?
- What are your objectives?

Currently, the most popular **Social Media Marketing** tools include:

- Facebook
- LinkedIn
- Pinterest
- Twitter
- Instagram
- Blogging

17.
MONEY, WHO NEEDS IT?
YOU DO IF YOU WRITE A BOOK

"Most authors don't see a return on their investment for a year or more."

Penny C. Sansevieri - Author

Early on, develop a realistic budget and contingency fund.

Don't spend the:

- House note
- Car note
- Tuition note
- Baby's formula note
- Other notes related to daily living

There is a cost factor to most everything you do and many things that you fail to do.

Just recently, I closed an unneeded, rarely used, overdrawn bank account. The cost, $100 hard earned dollars.

If I had responded when first notified, it would have only cost $20.

And so it goes.

And so it is with the craft of writing. The art of turning nothing into something, hopefully, something worthwhile.

Personal Resources

Be realistic about how much money you have to spend; and assess whether you can afford to lose it all if no one buys your book.

Learn about what kinds of goods and services you are going to need. Some have already been discussed.

Learn to negotiate, while understanding that some things are non-negotiable. Costs for copyright registration, ISBN, and other payouts are what they are.

You know you will spend money on graphic design, printing, and other items associated with the production, publishing, marketing and distribution of your book.

So be prepared.

Unless you've lost your mind somewhere in this process, **do not, I repeat, do not borrow from friends or relatives.**

Even if you pay them back in a timely manner...Even if your book becomes a runaway **New York Times** Best Seller...Even if, even if...

Don't do it.

If you do, your debtor will forever be blabbing about how they helped you become successful. How you couldn't have done it without them. Blah, blah, blah...

They will forever remain the unlanced boil, the appendage you wish you could sever.

Don't do it.

We have already discussed some of the obvious costs related to design, printing, marketing, legal, and, possibly, agent fees, if you choose that route.

Other controllable costs include those related to:
- Use of color
- Size of book
- Quantity
- Soft or hard cover
- Quality of paper
- Weight of paper

But, remember, when it comes to color, less is best for your budget, not necessarily for your book.

In some cases, recycled paper looks as good as new. I've seen finished products where only the cost revealed that the paper was recycled.

Try to keep costs reasonable at every step in the process.

Remember, people will not buy or review a cheap looking book.

So far, except for the following you have paid very little to produce your book.

- Paper
- Print cartridges
- Flash drives
- File folders
- Computer maintenance
- Gas

Your out-of-pocket expenses have been minimal.

That train is about to leave the station.

Be aware that much, if not all, of your expenses are tax deductible as costs of doing business. Make sure you follow IRS regulations in order to avoid problems. Satisfying IRS requirements is discussed in more detail in **Chapter 20** of this book.

Publishing Costs - A Brief Discussion

We are now ready to confront the next tier of costs before your book hits the streets.

Fortunately, there are many sources available, offline and online, to give you a realistic view of what to expect.

Consult the Internet to review a lot of information quickly. The explosion of interest in publishing, especially self-publishing, has resulted in all the information you need being available online.

For example, check out www.GoPublishYourself.com. There, you will find a cost guide focused on three of the major cost factors associated with publishing. Remember these are just estimates which can vary with the source, dimensions, and variations of each book.

- Editing - 1.5 cents per word
- Book Design (cover) $500 - $1,500
- Printing - Three separate estimates (see next page)

Printing - A Broader Explanation

The printing estimate, by necessity, requires more discussion than the other two services. Printing, aside from marketing, is the most complex process associated with publishing.

The following estimate assumes a quantity of 1,000 books, using a full-color or four-color process.

	Paperback	Hard Cover	Children's
Pages	192	192	32
Text	Black	Black	Full-Color
Paper	#50 White Offset	#60 White Offset	#80 Gloss
Color	Full-Color	Full-Color	Full-Color
Price Per	$2.71	$4.94	$4.92
Total Price	$2,710	$4,940	$4,920

Types Of Printing

The older you are, the more familiar you're likely to be with traditional ink-to-paper printing, also called offset. Typical minimum run for this process is 1,000 to 3,000, although you might find a smaller printer, anxious for the business, who might go as low as 100 copies.

This is especially true if the printer is **non-union** and used to dealing with smaller accounts on a budget.

Beware of non-union printers who pose as union printers.

The **union bug**, prominently displayed, will separate bonafide union printers from others. This is important to know because union printers typically charge more and you can usually be assured that they stand behind their work.

There are two other types of printing with which you need to become familiar.

1. **Digital** - Usually for short runs of up to 500.
2. **Print-on-Demand - (POD)** - This process is useful when an author or publisher doesn't want to maintain a large book inventory. POD literally allows you to print a book once it has been ordered.

In fact, you can contract with some vendors who will process the order, deduct their fee, and send you the balance. This typically costs more per book, than the other two processes.

Be on notice that your cost-per-book usually increases, the fewer books you print, whatever the process.

Closing Thoughts

Constantly review your budget, adjusting as necessary. If not, one day you'll quickly discover that you've overspent. Governments, and to a lesser extent, larger businesses can get away with this; but, small, startup businesses can't.

Remember, even if you self-publish, once you get into the production and publishing end, you are running a business. Even if you haven't done all of the necessary tasks to establish your business the right way, you are still in business.

It's to your advantage to set up legally and properly. That's the only way you can take full advantage of all available tax deductions and exemptions.

17. Money, Who Needs It? You Do If You're Going To Write A Book

18.
HOW DO YOU GET YOUR BOOK REVIEWED?

"Reviews sell books. They are the least expensive, most effective promotion you can possibly do for your book"

Dan Poynter - Author
"Dan Poynter's Self-Publishing Manual"

Most beginning writers give little thought to the possibility or importance of getting reviewed by a credible reviewer.

When and if the subject comes up they usually think only of outlets like the prestigious *The New York Times Book Review,* and little else. The truth is, regardless of your book's subject, there is an appropriate publication somewhere interested in reviewing that subject.

Keys to getting your book reviewed include:
- Sending a well-written book for consideration
- Sending it to the proper reviewer(s)
- Sending it at the right time

It also helps if you have followed the format and rules required by each reviewer.

If thought is given to the book review process at all, it usually focuses on the retail market, as represented by the already mentioned *The New York Times Book Review, Los Angeles Times Magazine,* and *Chicago Tribune Books,* also major reviewers.

Be aware of other opportunities, especially if you plan to self-publish.

There is another category of book reviewers who focus on the wholesale market, including book stores and libraries.

They include *Publishers Weekly* directed at:
- Book stores
- Wholesalers
- Libraries
- Publishers

Library Journal is geared toward **public libraries** that have **general collections**.

Whatever your total press run, make sure you allow for ample review copies. A review by a top notch publisher is the best promotion, and least expensive exposure, you can get for your book.

Plus, it's free.

Even if the review is unfavorable, some people will buy the book anyway because they don't believe in substituting a reviewer's opinion for their own.

Just getting your name out there as the author of a book can't be anything but good for you.

Dan Poynter's *Self-Publishing Manual* includes an excellent section on the mechanics of securing a book review.

Poynter recommends assembling a book package which includes:
1. **Book** - Should be brand new, preferably hard cover. If you send a soft cover book, then the reviewer might assume that the book has been out for a while. Most reviewers are

only interested in reviewing new books, preferably before they are published and distributed.

2. **Review Slip** - This contains all relevant bibliographic information about the book.

3. **Sample Review** - If you haven't been blessed yet, then write a review as a news release. Some smaller reviewers actually print verbatim if the news release is well-written and actually reflects what's to be expected from reading the book.

4. **Send Other Reviews** - Recognition lets a reviewer know that not only does your book deserve attention, but it also has already been recognized.

5. **Cover Letter** - Poynter feels it is unnecessary as long as the reviewer understands that the book is a review copy. This means that it must be clearly marked as such. My own feeling is that a short, well-crafted, to-the-point letter won't hurt.

Judith Appelbaum, in, **How To Get Happily Published,** offers the following astute observations about the reviewing process.

"Once you have copies and comments to distribute, be careful not to mail them out too early or too late. Check lead times for review organizations you hope will cover your work, and arrange to deliver it a month or two before the editors finalize the issue whose publication date coincides with yours."

"Remember, send galleys-not bound books-to **Publishers Weekly, Kirkus Reviews, The New York Times Book Review,** *and powerful monthlies that pride themselves on running reviews either before a book comes out or right around the publication date."*

I recommend that, once you see the direction in which your book is headed, you research publications - online and traditional - that are likely to have an interest in your book.

Find out their submission guidelines and follow them to the letter. If they want a finished book, send them a finished book. If they request galleys, send them galleys.

18. How Do You Get Your Book Reviewed?

19.
WHAT DO YOU NEED TO KNOW ABOUT THE LAW?

"Being prone to attack does not mean the investigative reporter is vulnerable, if caution is taken and the law is understood."

William Gaines
Two-time Pulitzer Prize winner for Investigative Reporting

In real life, "Ignorance of the law is no excuse." The same is certainly true of those who write for publication. As important as the law is in everyday life, few give it a second thought as they conduct their daily business.

Think about it.

When you wake up, you shower before putting on clothes and going outside, a legal necessity in most jurisdictions. Before going outside you will probably eat and drink something. The food you eat and whatever you drink is regulated by some governmental agency, like the Food & Drug Administration (FDA).

You get into your car, which has a state-registered license plate, and, most likely, a local sticker of some sort ... Before you hit the streets you make sure you have your driver's license, insurance card, and latest registration card for your car.

All of the aforementioned items are legal requirements.

You head for your job as a teacher, doctor, lawyer, or barber.

More legal requirements. And you haven't even arrived at work yet.

Get my point?

As an ordinary citizen, you deal with the law and its many requirements daily, even if you don't think about it. Fail to comply and you pay.

Trying to get on a plane to close that big business deal? Forgot your photo ID?

Fuhgetaboutit!

Writers-even more than the average citizen-must be vigilant in complying with the law. Failure to do so could render you broke and busted. Make a wrong move and you could end up on the street.

Already on the street, living in your car? You could end up on the curb, carless.

Quick Review: Plagiarism & Source Attribution

Plagiarism is taking credit for someone else's work. This is a big problem, particularly for students, educators, and, yes, writers. Sometimes it is an innocent act, unintended by the perpetrator.

Yeah, right.

No, really. It is possible a person could do so much reading and research that ideas as well as information run together and he actually thinks that someone else's work is his. It could really happen.

Nothing blows your credibility, whether student, educator, writer, or other, than being accused of **Plagiarism**, even if you are later found to be innocent.

Even as renowned a scholar as Dr. Martin Luther King, Jr., took a major hit to his academic reputation when it was reported that he had plagiarized portions of his doctoral thesis while at Boston College.

Even as I write, I cannot independently recall how that turned out. That's how devastating those charges are once made, whether true or not.

Avoiding Plagiarism

1. When in doubt, leave it out.
2. Always attribute sources.
3. Republishing plagiarized material does not protect you.
4. Getting author's or copyright owner's permission is the best protection.

Caveat: Make sure the person giving you permission is the actual author or owner of the copyrighted material.

Quick Review: First Amendment & Freedom of Speech

The **Constitution** is a great legal and political document, laying out in broad strokes the rights of the people, the reach and limitations of government, what is and isn't allowed.

Most people, many of whom haven't even read the **Constitution**, are quick to assert their rights under the document or, at least, what they believe their rights to be.

Many people are under the mistaken notion that the **Constitution** offers them unlimited rights. On any given night, on any street corner in America, you are likely to hear someone yell out the melodious phrase, *"F..k you."*

When the object of their affections responds saying, *"F..k you and your momma, too;"* a brouhaha is likely to ensue, ending in the arrest of one or both parties.

Both sides are likely to assert, *"I can say what I want to say. The Constitution gives me freedom of speech."*

Well, kind of.

It is extremely important that writers, who are hoping to publish, understand that what the **Constitution** gives, it also **restricts**.

Rabble Rouser, Tammy Terrible and **Ed Editor** found this out the hard way. Make sure this doesn't happen to you.

Rabble Rouser, a witty fellow, was attending the theater with friends.

As a joke he suddenly yelled, "Fire!," at the top of his lungs. The theater quickly emptied. Rouser, later charged with malicious mischief, claimed the **First Amendment** protected his speech, that he couldn't be prosecuted.

Tammy Terrible, en route to work, got into an argument with a bus driver, about the change she received.

The dispute escalated when she hurled a string of obscenities at the driver who was originally at fault.

The fracas ended when a police officer hauled Terrible from the bus and charged her with disorderly conduct.

Terrible claimed that the **First Amendment** protected her uncharacteristic conduct.

Ed Editor wrote a scathing article about a local politician whom he loathed.

The article claimed the politico had an unsavory background, police record, and associated with known gangsters. None of this was true.

The politician sued for **defamation**.

Caveat - The First Amendment protects most speech which encourages communication and the exchange of ideas.

Each of these cases illustrates speech not designed to communicate, but alienate. Falsely shouting *"fire!"* in a crowded building is action, not speech, and, thus, is unprotected by the **Free Speech** clause.

Obscenities are considered *"fighting words."* They encourage action, not communication, and are unprotected.

Defamation is a false statement that holds one up to hatred or ridicule. Courts usually require proof of injury like loss of income, before damages can be recovered. Because the politician is a public official, he is held to a higher legal standard, **(actual) malice**, to prove his case.

Defamation is either spoken (**slander**) or written (**libel**).

Caveats:

1. Freedom of Speech is a limited right.
2. The Free Speech Clause protects most communicative speech.
3. Some speech is considered action and, therefore, unprotected.

The First Amendment does not protect:

A. Obscenities

B. Defamation, slander or libel

Defamation - Broadly defined, defamation must harm one's reputation; expose that person to shame or ridicule; and result in some measurable loss, usually money. There are two basic types of defamation:

1. **Libel,** written defamation
2. **Slander,** spoken defamation

Example - You write a novel about a bank president who embezzled on such a large scale that not only did he bankrupt his bank, but also his entire network, including the holding company that owned the bank.

You present this as fiction and receive a huge advance. The book is published and makes all major best seller lists. Everyone lives happily ever after.

Not so fast.

Problem - There has been a real case with similar facts. The president has already been arrested, tried, and acquitted. He is just getting his life back together when your novel hits the best seller lists.

Your novel is not only similar, it also includes facts not presented at trial. Facts that someone could assume might be known by an insider. Since your book has such detail (because of your excellent research), people assume that insider could be you.

The new job being negotiated by the former president is suddenly withdrawn. Other financial deals that would have helped him restore his financial resources are quickly tabled.

Law enforcement starts showing up again at the house that he is just barely hanging onto.

And then, **he sues you for defamation**.

What now? First, set aside a sizable chunk of your royalties. **Defamation** suits can be difficult and costly to defend.

Defamation has five elements, all of which must be present for the charge to stick.

1. **Defamatory content**
2. **Publication/Broadcast**
3. **Identification**
4. **Fault: a. negligence b. actual malice**
5. **Harm**

1. **Defamatory Content** - The language at issue is untrue. Truth is the main defense against defamation charges.

2. **Publication/Broadcast** - Language must be disseminated to

at least one third party, someone other than the person claiming defamation and the person who wrote or spoke the words.

3. **Identification** - Person claiming defamation must be identifiable. Even if not identified by name, if a reasonable person could determine the identity, identification can be satisfied in some instances.

4. **Fault** - Refers to the two different standards used for the two main categories of those claiming defamation.

   A. **Negligence** - Private citizens must prove that someone failed to exercise the duty of ordinary care. Proof of negligence could be a simple failure to double check facts before publishing or broadcasting. It could be failing to check a statement by someone who doesn't like the claimant or by someone who has something to gain.

   B. **Actual Malice** - Often referred to simply as malice. A more difficult standard of proof used for public officials and public figures. The two categories of public figures include:

   • **General Purpose Public Figure** - Those whose celebrity makes them permanent objects of public curiosity. President Barack Obama, Michael Jackson. Either of the former Presidents Bush, Rosa Parks, and Madonna all qualify.

   • **Limited Purpose Public Figure** - Those who only enjoy a fleeting moment in the public eye. For example, the private citizen who drags a pregnant housewife from her burning car before it explodes.

The theory is that because public officials and celebrities are constantly in the public eye, more is written and said about them. Because it is more likely that a simple act of negligence might occur in their situations, they are held to a higher standard of proof, malice, to prove their case.

It is sometimes known as *"a reckless disregard of the truth."* You knew that what you were going to broadcast or print was likely to be not only untrue, but **defamatory**, and you printed or broadcasted it anyway.

This is a very high and difficult **standard of proof**. Celebrities rarely win defamation suits, partly because the tabloids employ some of the most highly paid and skilled reporters and attorneys. **Nevertheless**, writers should beware.

It doesn't help your career or your bank balance to become embroiled in a **defamation** suit.

Even if you win, you lose.

5. **Harm** - This refers to the actual loss caused by **defamation**. In the case of the now former banker, he is easily able to show substantial financial loss resulting from **defamation** and subsequent damage to his reputation.

If he decides to go for **punitive damages,** and wins, **your personal assets** could be at risk.

Including words like **alleged** or **reported** do not protect you from defamation. Also, be careful that you do not **republish** or **rebroadcast** a libelous or slanderous statement or statements. Many writers believe that just because something is in a reputable publication like the *New York Times,* or *Wall Street Journal,* or broadcasted by respected outlets like *CNN* or *PBS,* that the material is safe.

Republishing or rebroadcasting libel or slander simply makes you an additional, potential defendant when the offensive material is Googled and your name pops up, again and again.

Remember, with today's technology, given all of the websites, blogs, and social media, if you are found guilty of defamation, you could be sued into the next century. You could end up so broke that all you are allowed to write is your name on a check to pay off your accusers.

So, be careful what you write or say!

Caveat - The First Amendment allows me to insult you, but not to defame you without paying the cost.

Group Defamation

A group can be defamed and take you to court. Write or broadcast, without documentation, that a professional association of financial analysts are frauds, manipulators, and thieves and see what happens.

Consult a good First Amendment specialist if this happens. It's likely that you are going to need a lot of money. You might as well go with the best.

If you plan on centering your writing career around testing the limits of the law of defamation, make sure your defamation insurance is paid up. Also, make sure you are covered by a reputable company. Be aware that this insurance is expensive and does not cover you in all situations.

Get Yourself Covered

Check the Authors Guild - www.authorsguild.org for a list of where libel insurance may be purchased.

If you are like most people, who seek to write out of a sense of wanting to enlighten others and make a little spare change, beware of the following words.

- Thief
- Fraud
- Bankrupt
- Prostitute
- Whore
- AIDS/HIV positive
- Idiot
- Impotent

Avoid statements that question a person's

- Honesty
- Integrity
- Professional competence
- Sanity
- Solvency
- Morality
- Social refinement

Commercial Defamation

Sometimes the question arises as to whether a company, business, or other inanimate object can be defamed. While **commercial defamation** is litigated less than defamation of a person or group, there are some cases.

While former Chicago Bear running back Walter Payton was best known for his prowess on the football field, he was also an astute businessman and restauranteur, lending his name and face to several eateries in the Chicago area.

Payton's Restaurant Sues Over E-mail

by Andre Salles
Beacon News

In 2008 Manny Maysonet claimed he found two flies in his salad at Walter Payton's Roundhouse restaurant, then used his city e-mail account to warn people away.

Now Roundhouse owner Scott Ascher is suing Maysonet for "greatly injuring" the Aurora (Illinois) restaurant's reputation. He's seeking in excess of $100,000 damages.

Maysonet, assistant director of the Aurora Economic Development Commission, admitted sending an e-mail to hundreds of City of Aurora employees after he says he found the flies in his salad.

Maysonet wrote that the Kane County Health Department would be conducting an "on-site investigation" into "several complaints" of flies in the Roundhouse meals.

But the suit says Maysonet did not contact the Health Department until the next day.

The Health Department conducted an inspection and gave the Roundhouse high marks - 90 out of 100 and "minimal" flies.

But Ascher said the damage had been done. He said he began to see sales drop after the news hit the papers.

Do you think Ascher will win? Apply the five elements of defamation and decide for yourself.

Article appeared in the Chicago Sun Times - August 16, 2009 - P. 12A.

Privacy

A careful read of the Constitution reveals that there is no listed **right of privacy**, although it is well recognized. The right has been found in several clauses of the **Bill of Rights**, the first 10 amendments of the Constitution.

The **Supreme Court** in 1957 recognized a rather sweeping right to privacy in the **Griswold** case finding that there is:

- An independent right of privacy found in the Bill of Rights
- Privacy is a **fundamental liberty** and protected by the **Due Process** Clause of the **14th Amendment**
- As a fundamental liberty, government must have a *"compelling state interest"* to invade one's privacy

A *"compelling state interest"* requires *"strict judicial scrutiny,"* a very high standard of review. The government must show that it will suffer **substantial harm**, if the right of privacy is not restricted.

Why is all of this legal blather important to you, the writer? Again, like defamation, failure to respect one's privacy can expose you to substantial monetary losses.

Bet that got your attention.

Typically, privacy cases fall into four categories.

1. Private Facts
2. Intrusion
3. False Light
4. Appropriation

1. Private Facts - Simply put, every person has the right to keep private information private. This is especially true when a person is a private citizen and has not made an intentional effort to put himself into public view.

As a writer, **newsworthiness** is your main defense. **Chesley B. Sullenberger, III,** better known as "Sully" the U.S. Airways pilot, who performed the miraculous landing of his jet on the Hudson River, saving hundreds of lives, is a good example.

Sully, previously a private citizen, has been the subject of international news coverage. In writing about him, you find some previously undiscovered, unpublished facts that puts him in a less than heroic light. Unless what you published has some news value, which could be considered in the public interest, you might be subject to a suit by Sully and his representatives, even if what you write is true.

The court will inquire into the newsworthiness of what you published or broadcasted and weigh that against the perceived public interest.

Now, your lawyer will argue that Sully is no longer a private citizen, but a **limited purpose public figure**, one thrust into the limelight for a limited purpose and limited time. Your attorney may also cast Sully as a **general purpose public figure**, forever in the limelight because of his heroic deed.

2. Intrusion - Protects your right to private, secluded moments. A good example is former ESPN Reporter, **Erin Andrews**, who was photographed nude, standing in front of a mirror in a hotel room. Her image was then electronically transmitted all over the world.

Her main legal argument is that she had an **expectation of privacy**. Her lawyer argued that a hotel or motel room should offer the same expectation of privacy as one's own home.

Now, if she had been walking around nude in the lobby, we would have a different legal situation. There is absolutely no expectation of privacy in the lobby of a hotel, motel, or any other public place.

3. False Light - Everyone has the right to be represented accurately before the public. This is yet another reason to ensure that you include **correct names, spellings, addresses** and other identifying information in anything that you write or broadcast.

Misidentifying anyone as participating in a crime, contracting a dreaded disease, committing financial malfeasance, or something comparably scandalous, or similar mistakes could cause you big problems. Just as with defamation, republishing or re-broadcasting bad information does not protect you.

The main defense to a charge of **false light** is **truth**.

4. Appropriation - Every person has the right to control and benefit from his own persona or likeness. You cannot legally sell fake or real silver or gold coins with the picture of Barbara Streisand, Muhammad Ali, or Barack Obama's children.

They have the right to any monetary benefits that are realized because of their celebrity. Now, you do have the right to cast and sell fake coins with your own likeness as long as you are not representing it as legal tender.

You have the right to the same benefits as Streisand, Ali and President Obama's children. The problem is that your likeness is probably not worth anything, except to you and a small group of friends and family. Even then, they're not likely to want to pay for the privilege of owning a molten image of your smiling mug.

In the case of a deceased person, the monetary benefits should go to their designated estate. So, all of you out there who are selling Michael Jackson t-shirts with the wrong death date… **Stop it,** you're breaking the law.

The main defense to a charge of **appropriation** is **written consent**. Just be sure the consent is given by the appropriate person, or their legal representative.

Violations of **private facts, intrusion** and **false light** must be **highly offensive** in order to be actionable in most courts of law. An **appropriation** violation can occur simply if you don't have written consent.

Copyright

Most writers don't realize that a legally protected **copyright** is created at the time the written material is developed.

Caveat - Even though the material receives protection at time of creation, it is important to register the copyright as soon as possible.

If a dispute ever arises between two people or entities, claiming copyright ownership, the one that is registered (or if both are registered, the one with the earliest registration date) wins the dispute.

What Gets Copyright Protection?

Copyright protection is given under the legal concept of **intellectual property**. Intellectual property laws also protect **trademarks, service marks** and **patents**. Original works protected include those that are **literary, dramatic, artistic,** and **musical** including:
- Poetry
- Novels
- Movies
- Songs
- Computer software
- Architecture

Copyright protection does not extend to:
- Facts
- Ideas
- Systems
- Methods of operation

Caveat - The way something is expressed might be protected.

Although created by an employee or consultant, any work created as a **"work for hire"** situation is owned by the employer.

How Long Is Copyright Protected?

Currently, a **copyright** is protected for the **life of the author, plus 70 years**. There are some situations where copyright protection is extended even longer.

For all questions and clarifications concerning registering and protecting your copyright, including fees, please contact:

Library of Congress
U.S. Copyright Office
101 Independence Ave.
Washington, D.C. 20559-6000
www.copyright.gov
(202) 707-3000
8:30 a.m. - 5:00 p.m. (M-F) EST

Fair Use

Fair use of copyrighted material is generally allowed for the following purposes:
- Critique
- Comment
- News reporting
- Teaching
- Scholarship
- Research

Scope of Fair Use

- Whether use is for education or not-for-profit
- Nature of copyrighted work
- How much is used compared to length of copyrighted work
- Effect use has on market value or potential market value of copyrighted work

Source - Sect. 107 - U.S. Code

For more information on Fair Use see - Sect. 107-118 of the U.S. Code.

Caveat - Although fair use is not considered copyright infringement, the law does not specify how much material can be legally used under this doctrine.

Therefore, it is advisable that you get advance permission from the copyright owner. If this ends up in court, simply citing the Fair Use doctrine will not necessarily protect you.

If permission is not asked and received, courts will look at not only how much material was used, but the context in which it was used.

If for any reason you cannot make contact with the copyright owner, or you make contact and get no response, then **consult an attorney who is a First Amendment expert.**

The U.S. Copyright Office will not decide any fair use disputes.

19. What Do You Need To Know About The Law?

20.

WHAT ABOUT THE IRS?

*"The government realizes that it takes an investment
to run a business, and allows self-publishers to deduct any
work-related expenses from gross income"*

GoPublishYourself.com

If you decide to self-publish, you should follow all of the steps required in your state to form a small business. After thoroughly reviewing several options, the following are the steps that **Information Plus Professional Services**, publisher of this book, took to form an **S-Corporation** in the state of **Illinois**.

1. **Developed a Business Plan** - The process involved in creating this document helped determine the best business structure, based on short-term and long-term goals.

2. **Researched Business Structure options** - An **LLC, partnership, sole proprietorship, corporation,** were among the options discussed with our attorney.

3. **Reviewed Guidelines** for compiling the **Articles of Incorporation.**

4. **Conducted Business Name Search** with the state of Illinois

5. **Completed On-Line** application process.

6. **Consulted Attorney** regarding proper filing in order to **classify business** as an **S-Corp.**

7. **Filed** as an **S-Corp** with the Internal Revenue Service, under the **supervision** of an **attorney.**

Check with your state to determine what you need to do. This is the only way you can take full advantage of the tax benefits afforded by the state in which you are doing business. Setting your business up legally also helps avoid many unforeseen problems often faced by small business owners.

After legally setting up your business, **review all applicable tax law forms, rules,** and **procedures**.

Then, **find a good tax advisor,** preferably someone familiar with the publishing business and, particularly, the self-publishing business.

Payments to your advisor should be mostly tax deductible. Plus, it pays to have a professional on board right from the start.

If something goes wrong, then you have someone to blame. Otherwise, it spells more out-of-pocket payout for you. Don't forget, when you mess up with the IRS, you will not only pay your original debt, but also penalties and interest as well.

When dealing with the IRS, **be honest and thorough**. Don't try to beat them at a game in which they are the experts.

Keep good books.

Save all receipts related to **the cost of doing business**.

If you send a proposal package to a potential editor, publisher, or agent, then **save receipts for the stamp, paper,** and **envelope**.

When trying to determine if something is deductible before calling your advisor ask yourself:

Is the expense a cost of doing business?

If the answer is yes, then file it and ask your advisor to verify later.

Wait until you have several items for your advisor to review before putting him or her on the clock.

Assume that, just like lawyers, most financial advisors consider themselves on the clock as soon as they pick up the phone.

Forms

If your business is a sole proprietorship, you will list your profit and losses on **Schedule C (Form 1040)**.

Partnerships and joint ventures use **Form 1065** or **Form 1065 - B**.

If your business is a corporation, then consult an accountant or tax advisor regarding the appropriate forms and schedules to use.

How does this pertain to writers?

Most books are authored by one or two people. However, **academic** and **scholarly** publications sometimes contract with different authors who have a particular expertise and can lend that expertise to a specific chapter. The same is true of **anthologies**.

You may also have a book that is authored by one or more people, where an editor is given separate credit and acknowledgement, like this one.

Each of these situations can give rise to different tax situations, the use of more forms, and adherence to more tax laws and regulations.

Don't wait until the tax situation gets messy, to bring a qualified tax advisor on board.

Publications

Consult the following IRS publications as needed or visit www.irs.gov:

334 - Tax Guide for Small Business

463 - Travel, Entertainment, Gift, and Car Expenses

525 - Taxable and Nontaxable Income

529 - Miscellaneous Expenses

542 - Corporations

547 - Casualties, Disasters and Thefts

587 - Business Use of Your Home

946 - How to Depreciate Property

20. What About The IRS?

21.
SHOULD YOU QUIT YOUR JOB & WRITE FULL TIME?

"It's cool to have a 9 to 5."

R & B Singer Bobby Womack
"The Traveler"

Given the pain currently being inflicted by this economic recession/depression, I would strongly advise you to follow Bobby Womack's advice.

If you've got a 9 to 5, keep it.

Make a special effort to keep your gig if it provides even halfway decent health benefits.

Don't put yourself in the position of so many people featured on CNN and elsewhere. It's so bad that some people have even tried pulling their own teeth, with pliers no less.

Ouch!

After this painful experience didn't work, this particular young man still had to go to a real dentist to finish the job.

Nothing beats a regular check made out to you. Even if you don't know how long it's going to keep coming.

Writer Penny C. Sansevieri warns, *"Remember, as you're waiting to hit the big time, you'll need a place to sleep."*

I'll be honest, by the time I left my last job I was bored. On a typical day, I spent the last two hours watching Judge Mathis and the local and national news, respectively. Afterwards, I packed my bags and went home an hour or so early.

Damn, I grew to hate that job!

In fact, I hated it so much that I moved all of my personal items out of my office, a full six months before I left.

And I had a job that other people coveted.

By the time I left, all I had to carry out was my Rolodex and a small TV.

That was some time ago and I've never looked back.

It hasn't all been easy.

I went through a brief period where I longed for my old job. Actually, I was longing for my old pay check.

It didn't immediately click that now I didn't have to leave home to watch Judge Mathis; I also had time to do what I had wanted to do for a long time, write full time.

Before the fact that I was free fully registered, I tried doing contract work with a couple of communication startups - Didn't work.

It was then that the reality of no regular paycheck, hours, schedule, or routine kicked in.

I went through a period of feeling sorry for myself. Fortunately, I was quickly jumpstarted from that loser mindset.

Now, here I am giving advice to you.

During this time of transition, I learned several lessons including:
- God helps you if you help yourself.
- Things are never as bad as they seem.
- You are your only obstacle to success.
- You can't keep reinventing yourself.
- Friends are sometimes unfriendly.
- There is a time to talk and a time to do.

So, now, I'm writing for a living. It's not just a vocation, it's also an avocation as well.

I began researching and writing my first book more than 15 years ago. It never got done.

I researched and wrote the first draft of this book, in less than 90 days.

What's the difference?
- I accepted and met a challenge.
- I am more focused.
- I have more industry knowledge.
- I have better writing skills.
- I am tired of starting and stopping.

I am lining up appointments to discuss:
- Cover & interior design
- Printing options
- Marketing
- Legal review
- Costs

I have also recently identified someone I think can help me revive and finish that 15-year-old project.

As I continue to monitor today's turbulent economy, my ego says that journalism and law degrees can put me back on someone's payroll, if it becomes absolutely necessary.

Meanwhile, I have made a successful transition as Principal and Editorial Director of my own communications business, Information Plus Professional Services. This has allowed me an opportunity to work with my wife, Faye, who heads the Educational Leadership component of the business.

Ego also informs me that those same educational credentials, plus professional and life experience, plus the entrepreneurial spirit, and the fact that I am smart and resourceful, are enough to keep me doing what I'm doing.

Plus, since I've had time to think, I've had to be honest with myself and admit that I never really liked anybody telling me what to do anyway.

In the final analysis, you'll have to decide what's best for you.

For me, as long as I don't have to chase down shopping carts in some parking lot, or balance myself on roller skates while delivering a combo meal at one of those drive-in diners, I'll be just fine.

21. Should You Quit Your Job & Write Full Time?

22.
IF YOU WEREN'T SUCCESSFUL THIS TIME, SHOULD YOU TRY AGAIN?

"Easy reading is damn hard writing."

Nathaniel Hawthorne

Whether you should try again if you are not successful this time depends on how you define success.

How are you defining success?

Webster's dictionary defines success as "a favorable or desired outcome."

Only you can answer the above question. What did you expect or hope would happen when you set out to write your first book?

- Satisfaction?
- Money?
- Fame?

All of the above?

Rewind your life over the last few months, or so. Has writing your book:

- Caused household problems?
- Put you in debt?
- Made you anti-social?

All of the above?

If, however, the time spent researching, writing and, hopefully, ultimately, publishing your first book, has been a time of self-discovery, then you might want to continue the experience.

The goal of this book has been to make the whole process more understandable, a little easier, and, ultimately, more fulfilling personally.

I have tried to be honest about what to expect.

I have also tried to avoid unreasonably raising your expectations.

Whatever your personal situation, you still have a life to live. That didn't change just because you decided to write a book.

Hopefully, you have been able to maintain:

- Household activities
- Family responsibilities
- Health necessities
- Recreational outlets

Hopefully, you have not become obsessed and frustrated. At its best, writing a book should be fun.

It should bring out the best in you, not the worst.

As I said much earlier, the whole process can even be therapeutic.

Should you give it another go?

Although only you can decide, I would say give it another shot.

If you read this book carefully and followed most of my advice, then it's going to be much easier the next time around.

22. If You Weren't Successful This Time Should You Try Again?

THE BEST RESOURCE GUIDE

You are only as good as the quality of your information sources. This holds true whether writing and publishing a book, or any other activity. That's why this part of the book is just as important as what you have already read.

I have noted some of these invaluable sources in the body of my text. This is not meant to be comprehensive. There are plenty of other sources out there, that are just as good, and maybe even better. I just haven't found them yet.

If you have, feel free to email me the information. I will review and consider including them in the next edition of this book.

I have tried to categorize resources so you'll have a good idea of when you need to access them. Some are not easily categorized. But I have done my best to simplify this process.

You may find, just as I did, that the post-writing experience, when you are doing internal editing, fact-checking, meeting legal requirements, and other activities, are just as time-consuming and intense as actually writing the first draft of your book.

I recommend that you begin this process as soon after completing your first draft, as possible. That way, you maintain the necessary intensity that it took to write the book in the first place.

GETTING YOU GOING

Inspirational Resources

I spend some time in the book talking about the difficulty of getting started writing and the variety of excuses that can stand in your way. We often give ourselves the best, although irrational, reasons for not taking action and starting things that we claim are important to us. Therefore, I recommend beginning each day with short inspirational and devotional readings.

These will help jumpstart you mentally and put you in a good mood. More importantly, engaging in regular, positive, activity at the beginning of the day helps to erase our reasons for not doing.

Two of the best **Inspirational Resources** I have found are:

1. the daily writer – Fred White – Writer's Digest Books

Daily brief stories about various aspects of the writing process. This collection is not only inspirational, but is also full of tips that writers can use. Read first thing in the morning, or just before you begin writing. Keep up by reading one each day. If you play catch up, then you might defeat the purpose.

Also see **the daily reader** – Published November 2009.

2. The Intellectual Devotional – David S. Kidder & Noah D. Oppenheim – Rodale

Not specifically devoted to writing. Still an excellent motivational tool. Covers seven fields of knowledge, one each day. Includes history, literature, visual arts, science, music, philosophy, and religion. Read every day and you'll end up smarter than you ever thought you could be.

GETTING YOU THERE

Writing Right

1. Guide to Good Writing – Editors of Writer's Digest – Writer's Digest Books

The best writing, from the best writers, published in the best writer's magazine, reviewing all areas of how to write well. Covers each decade from the 1920s on.

This is good stuff from the best writers and editors around. To be the best, learn from the best.

2. On Writing Well –
William Zinsser – HarperCollins Publishers

The ultimate guide for the **nonfiction writer**. Discusses everything you need to know, in a clear, easy-to-digest way. Demystifies the art of writing well. Originally copyrighted in 1976, now available in a special 30th anniversary edition.

GETTING PAID

1. Damn! Why Didn't I Write That? –
Marc McCutcheon – Quill Driver Books

If you're saying, "Damn! I Wrote That – But Nobody Bought it!" ...You need to read this book. Details how you don't have to be degreed, have extensive writing experience, or be published, to make hundreds of thousands writing nonfiction.

2. How To Write A Book Proposal –
Michael Larsen – Writer's Digest Books

If it seems like I'm a fan of Writer's Digest Books, there's a reason. They're good. Don't waste your time writing a book. Instead, pen a winning book proposal. Then get paid to write the book. Larsen shows you how.

3. How To Get Happily Published –
Judith Appelbaum – HarperCollins Publishers

This book has it all. Unlike similar books, it reviews magazine publishing, as well as book publishing. Excellent advice aside, the resources listed are worth the price of the book. Follow Appelbaum's recommendations and you will be happy. You will get published.

4. The Well-Fed Writer –
Peter Bowerman –Fanove Publishing

Enough said, tells you how to get fed. Gives a realistic portrait of the life of a Freelancer. The book does an excellent job discussing the business aspects of how to support yourself, without relying on a 9 to 5. You'll know if this life is for you after reading this book.

5. The Writer's Idea Book –
Jack Heffron – Writer's Digest Books

Nothing is worse than a writer who has no original ideas. As a reader, you're looking for something new or, at least, something with a different twist. Heffron backs me up with this book that clearly illustrates that ideas are everywhere. Read this book and you won't know which publishable idea to pursue first.

GETTING INFORMATION

1. American University Presses Directory –
The Association of American University Presses

If you plan to do any level of academic writing, get this book. It is a listing of all major university presses in the country and includes comprehensive contact information, acquisition editors and their specialties, and; information on academic interests.

2. The African Amercian Writer's Handbook –
Robert Fleming – One World Ballantine Books

Title notwithstanding, this book will help any writer seeking advice on writing, proposals, agents, self-publishing, and how to excel in promoting your book. It also covers writers' organizations and has information on African American literary and publishing figures.

3. Book Publishing Resource Guide – Marie Kiefer – Ad-Lib Publications

The best one-volume compilation of publishing resources, covering all aspects of the industry. Need information on how to distribute, where to market, where to find professionals and specialists, and where to find other publishing information? It's all here.

4. The Concise Columbia Encyclopedia – Editors – Judith S. Levey & Agnes Greenhall with Reference Staff of Columbia University Press

Don't have much budget? Don't have much space? Don't have much time? Get this fact-filled, easy-to use reference. The last word on authenticated facts.

5. The Essential Researcher – Maureen Croteau & Wayne Worcester – Harper Perennial – Division of HarperCollins Publishers

Another great thumbnail research aide for journalists and book authors. Authoritatively covers everything from government, politics, law, history, science, health, and technology. Sections on culture, sports, and how to access information. Journalist's notebook covers legal issues, writing, and grammar.

6. Find It Fast – Robert I. Berkman – Harper Perennial - Division of HarperCollins Publishers

Tells you where to go to find what you are seeking. Libraries, Internet, government sources and more. It's all here. Uncovers expert sources and reveals how to utilize them. Recognizes that the best friend of journalists, and other writers, is time, not money. The chapter on Trouble Shooting justifies the book's cost.

7. **Investigative Reporting for Print and Broadcast – William Gaines – Nelson-Hill Publishers**

If what you're seeking is in the public record, then this two-time Pulitzer Prize winning Investigative Reporter will help you find it.

8. **The New York Public Library Desk Reference – Editorial Directors – Sheree Bykofsky & Paul Fargis, Simon & Schuster, Inc. Publishers**

If you can't find it in the New York Public Library, you don't need it. This acclaimed one-volume reference makes it easy.

GETTING IT RIGHT

1. **The International Thesaurus of Quotations – Compiled by Rhoda Thomas Tripp – Harper & Row Publishers**

Authoritative quotes, by authoritative people, add immeasurably to any writer's credibility.

2. **Merriam Webster's Collegiate Dictionary – Merriam-Webster, Inc.**

No hype needed here. End arguments fast. This remains America's best-selling dictionary.

3. **Random House Word Menu – Stephen Glazier – Random House**

A different kind of modern reference that organizes words by subject. Writing about Classical Music? Find appropriate terminology in the **Classical Music** section. Writing a penetrating piece on the **Applied Arts?** Review that section to find what you need.

4. **Elements of Grammar - Margaret Shertzer (Classic)**

GETTING IT SOLD

1. **1,001 Ways to Market Your Books –
   John Kremer – Open Horizons**

   Hopefully, you won't need 1,001 tips; but, if you do, they're
   here. Kremer emphasizes that authors should take prime
   responsibility for making sure their books get in the hands
   of readers. And he shows you, yes, 1,001 ways to do it.

GETTING IT SELF-PUBLISHED

1. **Dan Poynter's Self-Publishing Manual –
   Dan Poynter – Para Publishing**

   Widely considered the "Bible" of self-publishing. Poynter
   flushes out every detail of the self-publishing process. He
   is so thorough you might be challenged to put the book
   down and start writing. Yes, it's that good. He also shares
   a wealth of free information for writers on his website
   www.parapublishing.com.

2. **Self-Publishing For Dummies – Jason R. Rich – Wiley
   Publishing, Inc.**

   If you have a serious interest in self-publishing, you'd be
   a dummy not to buy and read this one. Yes, I said it. And
   I mean it. This is an excellent reference that takes you
   through every step of the process. The well-illustrated text
   helps facilitate the journey.

WHAT ONLINE SOURCES ARE BEST?

1. All you need to check out is (yes, once again) **the Writer's
   Digest 100 Best Websites for Writers.**

2. Oh yeah, you might also want to check out, **The Savvy
   Book Marketer's Guide To Successful Social Marketing
   – Dana Lynn Smith – Available as an E-Book for $24 at
   www.AuthorSocialMarketing.com.**

AFTERWORD

Thank you so much for buying and, presumably, reading my second book.

If you've stayed with me this long, by now, you realize that I'm a pretty funny guy.

I am so sure that this book will help aspiring writers that I make this promise: If this book inspires you to write and publish your own book, then I will be first in line to buy a copy.

Just give me an acknowledgement somewhere in your book.

In fact, if a video camera catches you stealing this book, and you avoid arrest and manage to write and publish your own book after reading my book, I will still be first in line to buy your book.

But enough of that. This **Afterword** is about alerting you to the publication of my third book. Look for the title: ***Hood Notes: The Eclectic Reflections of an Educated Negro on Life, Liberty & the Pursuit of Happiness in America.***

Hood Notes is shorthand for Neighborhood Notes, you know, the Hood.

This book is a republication of some of my previously published magazine articles and includes plenty of new and irreverent reflections on what's going on today.

The idea is to give a different take on everyday subjects, sometimes humorous, sometimes serious…but always thoughtful.

For example, I may include a piece on my newspaper delivery person. Not that I've ever met him, or it might be a her, for all I know. However, I'm assuming it's a male.

For the last two years, I have subscribed to our two local daily newspapers. This provides an important convenience for me because I like to read the newspaper first thing in the morning, before sitting down for that day's writing.

My newspapers usually arrive between 4 and 4:30 a.m. How do I know this? Because the delivery guy's car is in bad need of a new muffler. So his arrival with the day's news usually wakes me from a deep sleep.

When delivery first began, I could count on arising each morning and walking to my driveway, confident that my newspapers would be waiting safe and sound. But lately, delivery has become somewhat erratic. On some days, both newspapers will be where they should be, just inside the driveway.

Lately, on some days, one newspaper is in the driveway, the other is in the street. On other days both papers are in the street.

It has become quite an annoyance because, technically, if the newspapers are in the street, they really aren't mine, anyone can claim them.

So far, no one has. Although someone did steal both of my newspapers on the day after Barack Obama was first elected president.

This obviously upset me. In fact, I'll come right out and say it. I was pissed off!

Thoroughly.

So now, I never know what the situation will be from one day to the next.

Why not report the guy you say? After all, I'm still billed for the papers whether they have tire marks on them, or not.

Well, there was a time when I would have reported the guy. I would have reported him without hesitation.

That was before we went into this global recession. A time when even people who are multi-skilled, multi-degreed, multi-lingual are without jobs.

You get my dilemma.

I'm not sure I want to be the guy who drops a dime on the newspaper delivery guy, causing him to lose his job in a global recession, some would say, depression.

I'm not sure I want to be that guy.

At least with him gainfully employed, however marginally, he has things to do at 4 o'clock in the morning.

What do you imagine he might be doing that early, after he loses his delivery job, once his new, jobless reality sinks in?

I'm not sure I want to find out.

At least now his badlyinneedofamuffler car keeps cruising past my house after he has dropped my newspapers in the street, or occasionally, near my driveway.

What now, after he has been relieved of his duties?

Now, he's got time on his hands. And it's all because I wanted my damn newspapers tossed into my driveway, instead of the middle of the street.

Now, will he take to parking his car in front of my house at 4 in the morning, when he otherwise would have been completing his paper route?

Well, I'd better give this some more thought. It's not like I can turn him in anonymously.

He'll know it was me.

Oops, it's almost 4 a.m. Time for today's delivery. Yeah, here he comes right on time.

And, yes, there he goes.

Yeah, I'd better give this some more thought. Maybe I'd better learn to live with it. Maybe it's not such a bad deal after all.

Delivery is still better than going to the store.

And if I do that, somebody might rob the store, while I'm there buying my papers.

I might get taken hostage, or worse.

Oh well. I guess I'm not all that inconvenienced, the more I think about it.

After all, it's not like I was on that plane to Minneapolis when the pilots got lost and flew 150 miles out of the way.

Now that's inconvenience!

Yeah, that's right, things could be worse.

In fact, I'll probably give the guy a couple of bucks at Christmas time.

At least he leaves the newspapers in the middle of the street in front of my house.

Ah, such are the times in which we live.

Look for **Hood Notes,** coming to a bookstore near you!

CO-EDITOR ATTY. PATRICE N. PERKINS - is the owner of Lifestyle Zen, a law firm serving creative entrepreneurs, and an attorney for creative entrepreneurs, risk takers and dream makers. Her practice includes business set-up and maintenance, transactional law and intellectual property. She serves clientele who span all creative industries.

Dubbed the "creative attorney," Patrice understands the unique needs of creatives. In addition to direct services, she offers a workshop series: Real Law for Creative Entrepreneurs to educate creatives on the real law that they need to successfully transform their craft from hobby to business. Patrice furthers her mission to support creative communities through her non-profit organization, StreetFood Artistry.

Patrice is a regular presenter on legal topics addressing the needs of creative entrepreneurs. She enjoys providing counsel to help them protect their businesses, brands and long-term sustainability. Patrice is a graduate of DePaul University College of Law in Chicago, and Florida A&M University in Tallahassee, where she received a B.S. in Business Economics. Patrice is a recent contributor to the book, The Entrepreneur Within You, published by 220 Publishing.

Website: www.thelzgroup.com
Blog: www.mylifestylezen.com
Email Address: pperkins@thelzgroup.com

CO-EDITOR MICHELLE THOMPSON - a Chicago native, began her professional writing, editing, and consulting career immediately upon graduating from the University of Illinois College of Law. She was a writer, editor, and contributor at CCH, a Wolters Kluwer business, which is a leading provider of customer-focused tax, accounting and audit information, software and services for professionals in accounting firms and corporations.

Later, Michelle would serve as the Director of Operations for Francorp®, the foremost international management consulting firm specializing in franchise development. During this time, she not only worked with hundreds of clients to help them achieve their expansion goals, but she also developed business systems, operations manuals, training programs, and marketing materials for companies in a variety of industries.

Today, with more than a decade of experience, Michelle is an independent writer and business consultant. Most recently, she co-authored Groove Phi Groove Social Fellowship, Inc.- Black & White Works, The First 50 Years: 1962 – 2012 (Second Edition), which documents the history of Groove Phi Groove Social Fellowship, Inc., a social fellowship founded at Morgan State University in Baltimore, Maryland.

You may contact Michelle via email at thompson-m1@comcast.net.

Made in the USA
Charleston, SC
20 October 2013